God's Daily Word

Jerry Stratton

Armonia Publishing

ISBN: 1944613226
ISBN-13: 978-1-944613-22-8

DEDICATION

I dedicated book one of this three-book series to Dotse, my precious wife of 62 years. Book two was dedicated to our two wonderful children. Now, it is with great pride and tremendous joy that I lovingly dedicate this Book three to our six fantastic grandchildren: Bethany (husband Brian); Elizabeth (husband Aaron); Courtney, Christopher, Emily (husband Billy); and Erin. Also, I'm including our first great-grandchild, Georgia Mae.

"Grandchildren are the crowning glory of the aged; parents are the pride of their children" (Proverbs 17:6 NLT).

CONTENTS

ACKNOWLEDGMENTS

I want to acknowledge each person who suggested and encouraged me to undertake this three-book writing project. Thank you for both your prayers and encouragement during this spiritual journey. Also, I gratefully acknowledge all my fellow ministers and lay-people whose writings, sermons, life examples and testimonies have inspired me to undertake this project. Through these books, I pray many will be drawn by God's love into a saving relationship with Jesus Christ and that Christians will be strengthened each day in their journey toward spiritual maturity.

"But encourage one another daily, as long as it is called today, . . ."
(Hebrews 3:13 NIV)

Sep 01

Chuckle: *"You know it's going to be a bad day when you turn on the news, and they are showing escape routes out of the city!"*

Quote: *"If we refuse to be used by God, we may be used by the godless."* ~ William Arthur Ward

Apostasy: Its Consequences

"God gave this unchanging truth once for all time to his holy people. I say this because some godless people have wormed their way in among you, . . . The fate of such people was determined long ago, for they have turned against our only Master and Lord Jesus Christ. . . How terrible it will be for them! . . . They are like wandering stars, heading for everlasting gloom and darkness" (Jude 3b-4,11,13b NLT).

The word "apostasy" refers to a rebellion against God and His truths, originally instigated by Satan, the apostate dragon (See Job 26:13). It also means the intentional disregard for the truths of God's Word, and substituting one's own erroneous interpretations. The most dangerous apostasy for the church comes from those who know the truth, but are lured away by false teachings, and then feel it is their duty to discredit God and His church. Apostasy emerges from within the church when we begin to value worldly views more than Biblical truths.

An apostate's defection from the faith may be intellectual, perhaps from one's materialistic world view which leads to renouncement of Christianity and the church; or it may be moral and spiritual, as with Judas Iscariot, who for money betrayed his Lord. Apostasy can also be a subtle and creeping spiritual disease among Christians—a compromise here and a compromise there. At other times it leads to a sudden and total abandonment of Christianity. Apostasy is a constant danger to the church and there are many warnings about it in Scripture. Jesus warned about apostasy in the last days. *"At that time many will turn away from the faith and will betray and hate each other, and many false prophets will appear and deceive many people"* (Matthew 24:10-11 NIV).

A person can become convinced that God's Word isn't believable or doesn't make sense to his carnal mind; therefore, he declares it untrue. If the apostate is a smooth communicator who preys on those not well founded in the Word, he can lead in a gradual erosion of the sacred tenets of Christianity. The result can be a watered down gospel and a church operating outside of God's will.

There are many examples of apostasy: denial of the deity of Christ; denial of the virgin birth; denial that salvation is by grace through faith in Jesus Christ and nothing else; denial that Jesus died for our sins and rose again the third day; denial that Jesus will return to earth for a second time to claim His church, etc.

If we call ourselves Christians, we must be careful not to let worldly influences draw us away from the truths of God's Word and lead us into apostasy.

Sep 02

Chuckle: *A children's Sunday School teacher asked her class, "Who defeated the Philistines?" One little boy said, "I don't know. I don't keep up with the minor leagues."*

Quote: *"The Bible is so deep that theologians can never touch the bottom, yet so shallow that babes cannot drown."* ~ Unknown Source

Why Study the Bible?

"The law of the Lord is perfect, reviving the soul. The statutes of the Lord are trustworthy, making wise the simple. The precepts of the Lord are right, giving joy to the heart. The commands of the Lord are radiant, giving light to the eyes. The fear of the Lord is pure, enduring forever. The ordinances of the Lord are sure and altogether righteous. They are more precious than gold, than much pure gold; they are sweeter than honey from the comb" (Psalm 19:7-10 NIV).

I wonder how many of us see the Bible as a treasure from God and study it accordingly. It was written over a span of 1500 years by hundreds of different writers including kings, peasants, poets, herdsmen, fishermen, scientists, farmers, priests, pastors, tentmakers, and governors. Under the guidance of the Holy Spirit, the various books were gathered together, and they tell one complete story of God's love, grace, mercy, and forgiveness without contradictions or inconsistencies. Just stop for a moment and let the significance of all this this sink into your heart anew.

"All Scripture is God-breathed and is useful for teaching, rebuking, correcting, and training in righteousness" (2 Timothy 3:16). *". . . .men spoke from God as they were carried along by*

the Holy Spirit" (2 Peter 1:20).

Listen to what some famous people have said about the Bible:

Abraham Lincoln: *"I believe the Bible is the best gift God has ever given to man. All the good from the Savior of the world is communicated to us through this book."*

George Washington: *"It is impossible to rightly govern the world without God and the Bible."*

Napoleon: *"The Bible is no mere book but a living creature which conquers all who oppose it. For thousands of years the forces of evil have tried to discredit, ignore, or destroy God's Holy Word—but to no avail."*

Andrew Jackson: *"That book, sir, is the rock on which our republic rests."*

Daniel Webster: *"If we abide by the principles taught in the Bible, our country will go on prospering, but if we and our posterity neglect its instructions and authority, no man can tell how sudden a catastrophe may overwhelm us and bury all our glory in profound obscurity."*

The worldly, secular, progressive view is that the above observations are archaic, irrelevant, and were made by less than enlightened men. But, for believers, such statements about God's Word only add credibility to a truth we assimilated into our hearts and minds long ago.

Sep 03

Chuckle: *Visitor: "Wow, you have a lot of flies buzzing around your horses and cows. Do you ever shoo them?"*

Cowboy: "Naw, we just let them go barefoot."

Quote: *"All that is good in you comes from God, all that is bad, spoilt and corrupt comes from yourself."* ~ Jean-Pierre de Caussade

Foolish Arguments

"Again I say, don't get involved in foolish, ignorant arguments that only start (quarrels) fights. The Lord's servants must not quarrel but must be kind to everyone. They must be able to teach effectively and be patient with difficult people" (2 Timothy 2:23-24 NLT).

We live in a culture where people seem to become more angry and vindictive each day. Some display the attitude that "if you don't agree with me, you are my enemy and I have every right to destroy you." When we become angry with someone, the issues of disagreement often become no longer important—then we begin to attack his or her character.

I've heard politicians use the expression, "the politics of personal destruction." We seem to be losing the ability to have civil discussions of differing points of view while respecting the value and dignity of the person who disagrees with us. Unfortunately, this problem is not limited to the political arena; it is alive and well among "God's people" in the church.

No doubt, there are people who are difficult to get along with—those who think their points of view are the only ones that matter. They seem to say, "don't bother me with the facts, my mind is made up."

As he was instructing young Timothy on the finer points of teaching, Paul saw arguments and quarrels with difficult people as a significant and destructive issue for Timothy and all Christians. Paul says patience and kindness are key to effective teaching and interaction with other people.

Isn't it interesting that *patience* and *kindness* are among the fruits of the Spirit along with *love, joy, peace, goodness, faithfulness, gentleness and self-control* (Galatians 5:22 NIV). If you find yourself leading a Bible study, preaching, or having a one-on-one theological discussion, remember to respectively listen to questions and opposing points of view and avoid foolish debates and arguments. If you project an attitude of love and kindness, those who oppose you will be much more likely to listen to what you have to say and perhaps be persuaded by the truth of God's Word.

Finally, as we think and pray about dealing with difficult people, we must be careful that we do not appear as difficult in the eyes of those we are trying to teach and influence for our Lord. Common courtesy goes a long way. . .

"Starting a quarrel is like breaching a dam; so drop the matter before a dispute breaks out" (Proverbs 17:14 NIV).

Sep 04

Chuckle: *"Sure, you can lead a horse to water; most folks can . . . but if you can teach him to float on his back, then you've really got something!"*

Quote: *"The devil is sincere, but he is sincerely wrong."* ~ Billy Graham

Sincerely Wrong

"I am the way and the truth and the life. No one comes to the Father except through me" (John 14:6 NIV). *"I am the resurrection and the life. He who believes in me will live, even though he dies; and whoever lives and believes in me will never die"* (John 11:25-26 NIV).

No doubt you have heard people rationalize something like this: "it really doesn't matter what one believes as long as he is sincere." My dear friends, nothing could be further from the truth. You can sincerely believe anything you wish and be sincerely and tragically wrong. For centuries, people sincerely believed the earth was flat, but they were sincerely wrong.

The words from the lips of our Lord Himself tell us there is only one source of truth and one way to receive forgiveness of sins and eternal life in heaven. Here are several truths to consider:

1. We choose our beliefs. *"They exchanged the truth of God for a lie, and worshiped and served created things rather than the Creator—who is forever praised. Amen"* (Romans 1:25 NIV). People tend to believe lies that reinforce their own selfish, personal beliefs. You can choose to believe a lie, or believe God's Word.

2. Beliefs govern our behavior. *"Above all else, guard*

your heart, for it affects everything you do" (Proverbs 4:23 NLT). Our hearts—feelings of love and desire—dictate, to a great extent, how we live. We always find time to do what we value and enjoy doing.

3. The world teaches false beliefs. *"Do not believe everyone who claims to speak the truth. You must test them to see if the spirit they have comes from God. For there are many false prophets in the world"* (1 John 4:1 NLT). We should never believe something just because someone says it is a message from God. Test it against what God really says in His Word.

4. False beliefs can cause emotional stress and unhappiness. *"You are truly my disciples if you keep obeying my teachings. And you will know the truth, and the truth will set you free"* (John 8:31-32 NLT). Christ is the source of all truth, the perfect standard of what is right. He frees us from the penalty of sin and deception by Satan.

5. God is the only source of reliable and eternal truth. *". . Though everyone else in the world is a liar, God is true"* (Romans 3:4 NLT). *"Heaven and earth will disappear, but my words will remain forever"* (Luke 21:33 NLT).

It really does matter what you believe. You cannot afford to be sincerely wrong. Your eternal destiny depends upon your personal relationship with the One who said, *"I am the way and the truth and the life"* (John 14:6). *"For it is by grace you have been saved, through faith (in Jesus Christ)—and this is not of yourselves, it is a gift of God—not by works, so that no one can boast"* (Ephesians 2:8-9 NIV).

Sep 05

Chuckle: *"No, the handle on your recliner does not qualify as an exercise machine."*

Quote: *"The function of prayer is not to influence God, but rather to change the nature of the one who prays."* ~ Soren Kierkegaard

Pray in All Circumstances

"Is any one of you in trouble? He should pray. Is anyone happy? Let him sing songs of praise . . . Therefore confess your sins to each other and pray for each other so that you may be healed. The prayer of a righteous man (person) is powerful and effective" (James 5:13, 16 NIV).

God didn't give all of us the ability to sing beautifully. He never intended for all of us to preach. He never intended for us to have the same spiritual gifts. But one thing He intended for every believer to do is pray. Prayer can change your life and the world around you. We can sing and we can preach without the power of God, but when we get alone with God to pray, we can't do it in a meaningful way without His power.

James was a man of prayer. He talks about it in chapter 1, chapter 4, and here in chapter 5. The main thrust of this passage is the power of prayer and its appropriateness in every life situation. It is said that James became known as "camel knees" because his knees became hard and calloused from spending so much time in prayer. I venture to say none of us prays as we should.

I understand that eight-ninths of the bulk of an iceberg is below the waterline and out of sight. Only one-ninth is visible above the water's surface. Our prayer-life should be like an iceberg, with about one prayer out of nine being in public group prayer and eight-ninths out of sight in our private prayer time.

When we dip our cup in the ocean of prayer, we come up with more than a cup full of blessing. Nancy Speigelberg put it this way: *"Lord I crawled across the barrenness to you with my empty cup, uncertain in asking any small drop of refreshment. If only I had known you better I'd have come running with a bucket."*

All situations call for prayer—whether we are experiencing happiness, trouble, or sickness. However, prayer is never a means by which God can be manipulated into doing our will. Faithful disciples accept God's answer to prayer whatever it may be. The same God that created all things, died, and rose again, will listen to us. He will respond as we talk together with Him in faith. This miraculous provision from God Himself grants us the privilege of talking and listening to the Almighty God of the universe in the name of Jesus. Wow!!

Sep 06

Chuckle: *"You know it's a bad day when you call your spouse and tell her that you'd like to eat out tonight, and when you get home, you find a sandwich on the front porch.*

Quote: *"The less I pray, the harder it gets; the more I pray, the better it goes."* ~ Martin Luther

Prayer and Healing, Part 1

"Is anyone of you sick: He/she should call the elders of the church to pray over him/her and anoint him/her with oil in the name of the Lord. And the prayer offered in faith will make the sick person well; the Lord will raise him up" (James 5:14-15 NIV).

The subject of prayer and healing became very personal for me when I dealt with a cancer diagnosis followed by two major surgeries. I became aware of the power of prayer in a fresh and comforting way as I prayed, and as many brothers and sisters in Christ prayed with me and for me. If you've experienced something like this, you can understand my feelings.

James says we should pray when we are physically sick. He is also talking about times when we may be too sick and weak to pray because of serious life-threatening illnesses. When you are in this situation, James says you should call the leaders of the church together for prayer.

Anointing with oil was a first century custom (See Mark 6:13, Luke 10:34). Oil was used both for medicinal reasons and as a symbol of God's healing power. But the medicinal use of oil is not the issue here. Being anointed is to be symbolically touched with oil—not rubbed in, poured on, or taken internally as a medicine.

The oil symbolizes the healing power of the Holy Spirit. However, the main teaching is that healing comes through prayer, not the oil. Today, Christians should pray while using all available medical treatments—always trusting the Great Physician to bring healing.

We have seen people healed when we prayed, while others have died. We are reminded that we serve a sovereign God whose ultimate will is expressed in His decision whether or not to heal an illness. We should pray in faith and trust in Him.

"Healing is one of the most striking manifestations of the redemption of our bodies which salvation will bring, but it is an anticipation graciously and mysteriously vouchsafed to some and, equally graciously and mysteriously, withheld from others." ~ John Gunstone

None of us has everything figured out about Divine healing. Some say God doesn't do miraculous healing today. Not true. But we must understand it is not God's will to heal everyone just because we want it to happen. We should pray but leave the ultimate outcome to God and His sovereign will.

Robert Lawford put it this way: *"Prayer is not getting our will done in heaven, but getting God's will done on earth."*

Sep 07

Chuckle: *"If you put a crouton on your sundae instead of a cherry, it will count as a salad."*

Quote: *"What cannot be questioned is God's willingness to heal and the provision He has already made for that purpose to be fulfilled."* ~ Colin Urquhart

Prayer and Healing, Part 2

"Is anyone of you sick: He/she should call the elders of the church to pray over him/her and anoint him/her with oil in the name of the Lord. And the prayer offered in faith will make the sick person well; the Lord will raise him up" (James 5:14-15 NIV).

There are basically four kinds of sicknesses addressed in the Bible:

1. Sickness leading to death. At some point illness or accident will take our lives regardless of our faith. There is a time to be born and a time to die. *"Just as man is destined to die once, and after that to face judgment, . . "* (Hebrews 9:27 NIV).

2. Sickness as discipline. When we rebel against God and dishonor Him, He may allow a sickness to bring us back to Him. In 1 Corinthians 11, the "Christians" were criticized for the way they participated in the Lord's supper—they were not genuinely worshiping God. Paul said *"That is why many among you are weak and sick, and a number of you have fallen asleep (died). . When we are judged by the Lord, we are being disciplined. . ."* (See vs. 30, 32 NIV). God disciplines those He loves (See Rev. 3:19).

3. Sickness for God's glory. John 11 says Jesus was going to raise Lazarus from the dead for God's glory. In John 9, a man was born blind. People asked: *"Who sinned that this man is*

born blind? Was it him or his parents?" Jesus said: *"Neither this man nor his parents sinned."* Rather, *"this happened so that the work of God might be displayed in his life."* It was to bring glory to God.

4. Spiritual sickness. We should pray when we are sick and hurting spiritually. *"Therefore, confess your sins to each other and pray for each other so that you may be healed"* (James 5:16 NIV).

Many of our physical illnesses are the result of sin. Of course, many are not. Alcohol and drug addictions destroy our bodies. Smoking and over eating also harm our bodies. In the same way, sins of resentment, anger, and bitterness can create spiritual sickness.

Someone may have sinned against or hurt you, but you sin when you harbor resentment and bitterness which literally destroys you spiritually and makes you spiritually sick. The cure for such spiritual illness is to ask God to forgive you for your bitterness, and then ask for forgiveness from the person toward whom you are bitter and angry. Release of such burdens to God in prayer will make you feel better spiritually.

Sep 08

Chuckle: *A little boy was overheard praying, "Lord, if you can't make me a better boy, don't worry about it. I'm having a real good time like I am."*

Quote: *"For the Christian, praying should be like breathing. Just as breathing is the response of physical life to the presence of air, so prayer should be the response of spiritual life to the presence of God."* ~ Unknown Source

Praying with Power

"The prayer of a righteous man is powerful and effective" (James 5:16b NIV).

According to Scriptures, there are certain principles which we must understand if we are to be righteous and pray with power.

1. Pray with a clean heart. Our first step in praying with power is to confess our sins and allow God to forgive those sins and cleanse our hearts and minds. Remember from our last lesson, *"If we confess our sins, he is faithful and just and will forgive us our sins and purify (cleanse) us from all unrighteousness"* (1 John 1:9 NIV).

2. We must ask. *"You do not have because you do not ask God"* (James 4:2 NIV). Ask for specific things in your prayers. "Lord bless all the Christians, heal all the sick, and save all the lost, and bless all the missionaries" is too general. We should pray for specific people and specific needs. God wants us to care for individuals—like Jesus did, and pray for them with love, concern, compassion, and persistence for their specific needs. Pray for the unsaved by name and with great burden. Jesus says to us, *"Ask and it will be given to you; seek and you*

will find; knock and the door will be opened to you" (Matthew 7:7 NIV).

3. Pray with the right motive. *"You ask and do not receive because you ask with the wrong motives, that you might spend what you get on your own (selfish) pleasures"* (James 4:3 NIV). After we have been cleansed and forgiven of our sins, and when we pray in accordance with God's will, self will be last on our prayer list and others will be first. We should not just pray for "me and mine," but pray God's heart with His kingdom in mind.

4. Pray in faith. *"But when he asks, he must believe and not doubt"* (James 1:6 NIV). Praying in faith is described in 1 John 5:15 NIV: *"This is the confidence we have in approaching God: that if we ask anything according to His will, he hears us. And if we know that He hears us—whatever we ask—we know that we have what we asked of Him."* Jesus said: *"If you remain in me and my words remain in you, ask whatever you wish and it will be given you"* (John 15:7 NIV). If we remain in Christ, we will never pray selfishly for anything contrary to His character or His will.

Jesus set the example for us by praying to His Father often and persistently. This truth was captured well by St. Cyprian who said, *"If He prayed who was without sin, how much more it becomes a sinner to pray."*

It is God's desire that our prayers be powerful and effective.

Sep 09

Chuckle: *"Some churches are now serving coffee after the sermon. Perhaps this to get people thoroughly awake before they drive home!"*

Quote: *"Sin is believing the lie that you are self-created, self-dependent, and self-sustained."* ~ Augustine

The Stain of Sin

"Come now, let us reason together," says the Lord. "Though your sins are like scarlet, they shall be as white as snow; though they are red as crimson, they shall be like wool" (Isaiah 1:18 NIV).

God has a way of communicating with us that leaves no doubt about His meaning. In the New Testament, Jesus often spoke in parables (a common story to communicate a deep spiritual lesson) using familiar references easily understood by His audience. These parables are sometimes called "earthly stories with heavenly meanings." Here through the prophet Isaiah, God used metaphors, which had clear meaning in the culture of that day to describe the sins of His people.

Crimson was the color of a deep-red permanent dye—a stain almost impossible to remove from cloth. The stain of sin seems equally permanent, but God can remove sin's toughest stain from our lives as He promised to do for the Israelites.

Earlier in this chapter, God had chastised His people for having blood on their hands because of the misery and injustice they brought upon less fortunate people. The bloodstains on the hands of murderers are probably the reference here: *"Your hands are full of blood"* (See vs. 15)

But we don't have to go through life permanently soiled

by our sins, regardless of their severity. We are assured in God's Word that if we are willing and obedient, Jesus Christ will forgive and remove our most indelible stains. *"Have mercy on me, O God, because of your unfailing love. Because of your great compassion, blot out the stain of my sins. Wash me clean from my guilt. Purify me from my sin"* (Psalm 51:1-2 NLT).

When we pray for forgiveness as did the psalmist, God has promised to *"forgive our sins and purify us from all unrighteousness"* (1 John 1:9 NIV). God wants to forgive and cleanse us. That's why He allowed His beloved Son to die—so He could offer us a complete pardon for our sins. When we come to Christ, He forgives all our past sins and we don't need to keep on confessing them again and again. They're gone forever! We never again need to fear God's rejection because of our sins. However, we must remember that true confession and repentance involves a commitment not to continue to sin.

Do you fully appreciate what it means to have your sins forgiven and the stain of those sins removed by the Creator of the Universe through faith in His one and only Son? We are wise if we take the time to just dwell on this truth and wallow around in God's love.

Sep 10

Chuckle: *A cop to an offender: "If you run . . . you'll only go to jail tired."*

Quote: *"I have so much to do that I must spend the first three hours of each day in prayer."* ~ Martin Luther

When Should We Pray?

"Is any one of you in trouble? He should pray. Is anyone happy? Let him sing songs of praise . . . Therefore confess your sins to each other and pray for each other so that you may be healed. The prayer of a righteous man, person, is powerful and effective" (James 5:13, 16 NIV).

We should pray when we are in trouble. This original Greek word translated as "trouble" means stress, difficulty, affliction, suffering. These are emotional stresses brought on by outward difficulties (finances, family, work, etc.). What should we do first? We should pray—even before we seek help from a friend, a counselor, parents, or pastor, etc. David quoted the Lord as saying: *". . . call upon me in your time of trouble; and I will deliver you"* (Psalm 50:15 NIV). We must come into God's presence so His power can be brought to bear on our problems.

We should pray when we are happy. Our prayers should take the form of songs of praise. *"Praise the Lord! Praise God in his Temple; praise him in his mighty heaven. Praise him for his strength; praise him for his greatness. Let everything that breathes praise the Lord. Praise the LORD!"* (Psalm 150:1-2; 6 NIV). Songs—sounds of praise—should rise to God spontaneously from the basic mood of joy which marks the lives of the people of God. God's attributes give us all the justification we need to praise Him—His love, mercy, power, majesty, presence, etc.

James is telling us that prayer of some kind is appropriate in all situations—whether we are troubled, happy, or sick. He is confirming the instructions of the apostle Paul to "pray without ceasing." This means we go through life in a constant attitude of prayer—constantly seeking God's wisdom in every situation. We should value our privileged communications with the Creator of the universe in the name of Jesus.

"Prayer pulls the rope down below and the great bell rings above in the ears of God. Some scarcely stir the bell, for they pray so languidly; others give only an occasional jerk at the rope. But he who communicates with heaven is the man who grasps the rope boldly and pulls continuously with all his might." ~ C. H. Spurgeon

Sep 11

Chuckle: *Father and son are watching television; "Dad, tell me again how when you were a kid you had to walk all the way across the room to change the channel."*

Quote: *"Goodness makes greatness truly valuable, and greatness makes goodness much more serviceable."* ~ Matthew Henry

Experiencing God's Presence

Jesus replied, "All those who love me will do what I say. My Father will love them, and we will come to them and live with them" (John 14:23 NLT).

There are times in our lives when circumstances cause us to question whether God's presence is still with us. When these thoughts come, they usually accompany a difficult time we are experiencing. We are tempted to ask, "God, if you're really here with me, why do you allow this to happen? Why can't I sense you with me?"

When we feel as if God has left us, more than likely it's because we have allowed some sin to enter our lives that has distracted us and caused us to move away from God, rather than His moving away from us. The Bible says, *"Draw close to God, and God will draw close to you. Wash your hands, you sinners, purify your hearts, you hypocrites"* (James 4:8 NLT). James gives us five ways to draw near to God and experience His presence anew:

1. *"Humble yourselves before God"* (See 4:7). Yield to His authority and will. Allow His Holy Spirit to fill and control your life—be willing to follow Him.

2. *"Resist the Devil"* (See 4:7). Don't allow Satan to entice

you, tempt you, and draw you away from Godly pursuits.

3. *"Wash your hands . . and purify your hearts"* (See 4:8). Be cleansed by confessing your sins (See 1 John 1:9), and lead a pure life. Replace your desire to sin with a desire to experience God's presence and purity.

4. *"Let there be sorrow and deep grief"* for your sins (See 4:9). Don't be hesitant to express to God your heartfelt sorrow for what you have done.

5. *"Bow down before the Lord, and he will lift you up"* (See 4:10; 1 Peter 5:6 NLT).

If you don't sense God's powerful presence in your life, remember Jesus' words in Revelation 3:20 to the church members at Laodicea: *"Here I am! I stand at the door and knock. If anyone hears my voice and opens the door, I will come in and eat with him, and he with me."*

Here Jesus is speaking to Christians and is desiring fellowship with them. Notice that Jesus does not assume that His knock or His voice are being heard. He says "if anyone hears my voice." We must actively seek Him and listen for His voice to fully experience His presence and fellowship with Him. You will experience God's presence daily as you look to His Holy Spirit for guidance in every circumstance life.

You cannot exclude Him from certain areas of your life and still sense His presence.

Sep 12

Chuckle: *A man goes to an eye doctor. The receptionist asks him why he is there. "I keep seeing spots," explained the man.*

The receptionist asked, "Have you ever seen a doctor?"

"No, just spots," replies the man.

Quote: *"Love is the child of freedom, never that of domination."* ~ Erich Fromm

The Law of Love and Freedom

"So whenever you speak, or whatever you do, remember that you will be judged by the law of love, the law that set you free" (James 2:12 NLT).

During my military career, I was an Army pilot and flew both helicopters and fixed wing aircraft. During my training, I became more keenly aware of the effects of gravity on our lives, especially as it impacts the loading and flight of aircraft. Everything we do physically is impacted by the law of gravity. As we exercise, our muscles are strengthened by repetitive exertions against the gravitational pull on our bodies. Gravity is a constant.

Think for a moment what life would be like without gravity. Flying would be easy but getting back on the ground would be a challenge. Food would levitate from our plates and liquids in our glasses would float out into the air. We would struggle to keep from floating off into space ourselves. Yes, life would be much different without gravity.

Likewise, life would be a lot different without the drawing power of God's love. Our lives would be a lot different were it not for the law of love that sets us free. Every day the constant law of love is at work as God demonstrates that love through His mercy and grace. His love is constantly tugging at our hearts, drawing us closer and closer to Him. God's law of love is no longer an external set of rules, but it is a *"law that sets you free"* when, by faith, you give your heart and life to Christ.

As the law of gravity keeps everything in order in our world, God's law of love keeps our spiritual lives in order. The most beautiful thing about this picture is that when we stand before Christ to be judged, *"we will be judged by God's (constant) law of love"* (2 Cor. 5:10). In our first passage, this truth is made abundantly clear. Yes, our lives would be a lot different without God's law of love that sets us free.

The challenge for us is to love others as Christ loves us. Jesus said, *"As I have loved you, so you must love one another"* (John 13:34b NIV). Our living out God's law of love and freedom is not optional, but an obligation. It is God's plan for us to radiate His love and be His instruments for drawing others to Himself. We should extend to others the same love, mercy, grace, and forgiveness that God has extended to us.

Sep 13

Chuckle: *A little boy was asked, "What is a lie?"*

The boy replied, "It is an abomination unto the Lord and a very present help in the time of need!!"

Quote: *"There is so much for us all to forgive that we shall never get it done without putting in a lot of practice."*
~ J. Neville Ward

Blessings from Forgiving

"Then came Peter to Him, and said, 'Lord, how often should I forgive someone who sins against me? Seven times?' 'No,' Jesus replied. 'seventy times seven!'" (Matthew 18:21-22 NLT).

Jesus taught that if we remain in Him and He remains in us, we can pray and receive whatever we ask (See John 15:7). He also taught us that we should pray and believe by faith. Then He states that if you have anything against anyone when you pray, forgive that person. If you hold a grudge, and refuse to let it go, the flow of blessings that God wants to give you will be interrupted. As long as such resentment and grudges are allowed to continue, God's forgiveness for you will be withheld as well.

Jesus said: *"Listen to me! You can pray for anything, and if you believe, you will have it. But when you are praying, first forgive anyone you are holding a grudge against, so that your Father in heaven will forgive your sins, too"* (Mark 11:24-26 NLT). Jesus spoke again on unwillingness to forgive and offensiveness when He taught the disciples how to be reconciled with a brother who had offended them. Peter thought he was being generous when he suggested we forgive someone seven times, but Jesus not only taught us how many times to forgive, but how to forgive—He modeled it for us.

Forgiveness is the act of pardoning an offender in spite of the offender's shortcomings and errors. It's the last thing Jesus did on the cross! With His life almost at an end and His body in total agony, He asked the Father to forgive His tormenters. *"Jesus said, 'Father, forgive these people, because they don't know what they are doing"* (Luke 23:34 NLT). When we exercise genuine forgiveness, we are freed from the most powerful bondage that the enemy can impose on us. *"You must make allowance for each other's faults and forgive the person who offends you. Remember, the Lord forgave you, so you must forgive others. And the most important piece of clothing you must wear is love. Love is what binds us all together in perfect harmony"* (Colossians 3:13-14 NLT).

Jesus didn't say we are to forgive when we feel like it. He said it is a duty and no limits can be set on the extent of forgiveness. It must be granted without reservation, by faith and not feelings. Regardless of the hurt, we are to forgive as God does, without limits.

You and I can never be free and happy if we harbor grudges, so put them away. Get rid of them. Collect postage stamps, or collect coins, if you wish—but don't collect grudges. Such ability to forgive will result in an outflow of blessings—peace, joy, and contentment.

Sep 14

Chuckle: *"Never put both feet in your mouth at the same time, because then you won't have a leg to stand on. . . .!!"*

Quote: *"Martin Luther said he only had two days on his calendar— today and that day (Rapture)."*

The Rapture of the Church

"*For the Lord himself will come down from heaven, with a loud command, with the voice of the archangel and with the trumpet call of God, and the dead in Christ will rise first. After that, we who are still alive and are left will be caught up together with them in the air. And so we will be with the Lord forever"* (1 Thessalonians 4:16-17 NIV).

Nowhere in Scripture do you find the word "rapture" as it relates to the second coming of Christ. It is a word coined by theologians, and adopted by most Christians, to describe the events surrounding the appearance of our Lord when He comes to take to heaven both dead and living believers who will make up His eternal church. The timing of the "rapture" remains a mystery and only the Father knows when Jesus will return.

I won't attempt to answer all the questions surrounding Christ's return, but I want to present some of the many Scriptures that confirm that He will return. Our understanding of Christ's second coming is expanded by the words of Jesus Himself: *"And if I go to prepare a place for you, I will come back and take you to be with me that you may be where I am"* (John 14:3 NIV). Here Jesus promises His followers that He will return to earth a second time to take us with Him to our eternal home in heaven—to a place He has prepared for all who believe in Him.

Concerning the timing of His return, Jesus said: *"At that time men will see the Son of Man coming in clouds with great power and glory. And he will send his angels and gather his elect from the four winds, from the ends of the heavens . . . No one knows about that day or hour, not even the angels in heaven, nor the Son, but only the Father"* (Mark 13:26-27, 32 NIV). Because of Biblical prophecies that have been fulfilled, we have strong indications that we may be approaching the time of Jesus' return. However, no one can predict with certainty the date and time of the glorious event.

In our primary passage, we are told that when Christ returns for His church, those believers who have died in Christ will be raised first and those who are still alive will be changed into their glorified bodies suitable for God's presence. *"Listen, I tell you a mystery: We will not all sleep (die), but we will all be changed—in a flash, in the twinkling of an eye, at the last trumpet. For the trumpet will sound, the dead will be raised imperishable and we will be changed"* (1 Corinthians 15:50-53 NIV). It's interesting to note that at the "rapture" Christ does not physically come to earth. Instead, we, in our glorified bodies, will join Him and all other believers in the air.

There are differing interpretations of Scripture concerning the exact sequence of events following the "Rapture" of the church such as the seven years of tribulation, Christ's return to establish His millennial reign, the Great White Throne judgment, etc.

Sep 15

Chuckle: *"Smartness runs in my family. When I went to school I was so smart my teacher was in my class for five years."* ~ George Burns

Quote: *"When God measures a person, he puts the tape around his heart and not his head."* ~ Unknown Source

Search Me, O God

"Search me, O God, and know my heart; test me and know my thoughts. Point out anything in me that offends you, and lead me along the path of everlasting life" (Psalm 139:23-24 NLT).

We do not know our own hearts well enough to search and test them for ourselves. David asked God to search his heart and mind and point out any wrong motives that may have been behind his strong words against his enemies. This request is important because *"The human heart is most deceitful and desperately wicked. Who really knows how bad it is? But I know! I, the Lord, search all hearts and examine secret motives. I give all people their due rewards, according to what their actions deserve"* (Jeremiah 17:9-10 NLT).

Our tendency is to want to examine our own hearts, but in our own strength, we are incapable of doing so by God's standards. If we sincerely ask God to examine our hearts, while studying His Word and praying, He will reveal secret motives, weaknesses and sins that we never knew existed. Have you ever acted in a sinful way, then asked yourself, "Why did I do that?" Your actions may be the result of some hidden motive that only God can reveal when you let Him do a thorough heart and mind search.

In a similar way, we may think we can make ourselves good enough to be acceptable to God by cleaning up our lives according to the best of our abilities. But God knows our actions mean nothing without a change of heart. *"Man looks at the outward appearance, but the Lord looks at the heart"* (1 Samuel 16:7 NIV).

God makes it clear that we sin based on the condition of our hearts. Our hearts are inclined toward sin from the time we are born. Even Christians can forget God and slip into sin, but to sin or not is our choice. We can yield our lives to Satan's temptations, or we can turn to God, confess our sins in repentance and allow God to cleanse and purify our hearts as He removes the motives for our sinful actions and words (see 1 John 1:9).

When people observe your life, does what they see accurately reflect the condition of your heart? It can—if you ask God to search your heart, as David did, and reveal any hidden motive or condition that offends Him and causes you to bring dishonor to His Name. Once God has cleansed your heart and forgiven you, then your joy will return in full measure.

Sep 16

Chuckle: *"Two men were shipwrecked and floating on a raft. One started to pray— 'O Lord, I've been an awful sinner all my days. Lord, if you'll spare me, I'll —'*

The other man shouted— 'Hold on, don't commit yourself —I think I see a sail!'"

Quote: *"All men desire peace, but very few desire those things that make for peace."* ~ Thomas à Kempis

Peace in a Chaotic World

"For the Lord is God, and he created the heavens and earth and put everything in place. He made the world to be lived in, not to be a place of empty chaos. 'I am the Lord,' he says, 'and there is no other'" (Isaiah 45:18 NLT).

Every day it seems our world sinks deeper and deeper into a chaotic state. Wars are raging and terrorists are killing innocent people around the world. All sorts of unreasonable violence occurs constantly. Adults are shooting kids. Kids are shooting each other. Parents are shooting their children and each other. Random violence is everywhere and the perpetrators seemingly have no remorse—no consciences.

What in the world is going on? One thing is certain, God is not the instigator of such chaos. We serve a God of peace and joy who wants us to live in serenity and happiness even in the midst of the chaos around us. How then can you find order and peace in your spirit during these troubled times?

As we seek to know our Lord God better each day—the One who created order and peace—He will fill us with His peace. It is your relationship with Jesus Christ that gives you peace. It is His gift to you, and He wants that peace to become more complete in your life every day as you follow Him. *"Since we have been made right in God's sight by faith, we have peace with God because of what Jesus Christ our Lord has done for us"* (Romans 5:1 NLT).

Everywhere you look, destructive forces seem determined to take away your safety, peace, and contentment. If you turn to the world for solutions, they cannot be found. It's only from your relationship and fellowship with God through Christ that the solutions become apparent. Troubles and chaos will always be found in life, which can threaten your peace of mind and spirit. To find inner peace in the midst of chaos, seek to better understand God's perspective on life. As your faith deepens, peace will come.

"Picture a massive hurricane raging over the ocean. On the surface of the sea the violent winds whip the water into giant waves and create a scene of havoc and chaos. Yet, a mere twenty-five feet below the surface, the waters are clear and calm. The fish there go on living their lives totally unaware of the thunderous tumult just above them. Where there is 'depth,' there is peace. So it is in the Christian life." ~ Illustrations for Biblical Preaching, Edited by Michael P. Green.

"May God bless you with his special favor and wonderful peace as you come to know Jesus, our God and Lord, better and better" (2 Peter 1:2 NLT).

Sep 17

Chuckle: *Boy: "Grandma, do you know how to croak?"*
"No, I don't think so. Why?"
"Because Daddy says he'll be a rich man when you do."
Quote: *"For I am not ashamed of the gospel of Christ: for it is the power of God unto salvation to everyone that believeth."*
~ Apostle Paul in Romans 1:16 KJV

Identified with Christ

"Whoever acknowledges me before men, I will also acknowledge him before my Father in heaven. But whoever disowns me before men, I will disown him before my Father in heaven" (Matthew 10:32-33 NIV).

If you have, or have had, teenagers in your home, you know many of them go through a stage, around 14 or 15, when they want nothing to do with their parents. They don't even want to be seen with them. They're too grown up for things like that. I've learned such conduct is not uncommon for teenagers as they struggle for personal identity in that troublesome time between childhood and adulthood known as adolescence.

Sadly, there was a close follower of Jesus who disavowed any connection with Jesus when He was taken into custody on the evening before His crucifixion. Earlier, Jesus had predicted that Peter, one of His closest disciples, would deny Him three times before the rooster crowed in the morning. Of course, Peter said he would never deny or disown his Lord. But as Jesus had predicted, when the going got rough, Peter denied he even knew Jesus on three separate occasions recorded in John, chapter 18. Peter's third and final denial went like this: *"One of the high priest's servants . . . challenged him, 'Didn't I see you with him (Jesus) in the olive grove (where Jesus was arrested)?' Again Peter denied it, and at that moment a rooster began to crow"* (John 18:26-27 NIV).

It is one thing for teenagers to temporarily fail to acknowledge their parents before their friends. It is another thing altogether for Christians to fail to acknowledge their Lord and Savior before those around them. Those of us who publicly acknowledge and identify with Christ have His promise that He will acknowledge us before His Father. Jesus left no doubt that there is no place for secret disciples. By every word we say and by every act we perform, we are to publicly confess Jesus Christ as Lord and Savior. Such public confession will reap eternal rewards. If our faith is not strong enough to cause us to be identify with Christ, we cannot expect God to be gracious with His rewards.

When the rooster crowed, it reminded Peter of the gravity of what he had done. Fortunately, Peter repented, was forgiven, and later became one of the strongest New Testament voices for his Lord. Maybe you have denied or disowned your Lord by words or actions. Maybe people have no clue that you are even a Christian because of your hesitancy to speak out and be identified with Christ. If so, you may need to bow before God and ask forgiveness and cleansing. Then, in the power of the Holy Spirit, identify with Christ at every opportunity.

Sep 18

Chuckle: *A three year-old kissed his Mom goodnight. "I love you so much, that when you die I'm going to bury you outside my bedroom window."*

Quote: *"As a well-spent day brings happy sleep, so life well used brings happy death."* ~ Leonardo da Vinci

How Do You Want to Be Remembered?

"As for man, his days are like grass, he flourishes like a flower of the field; the wind blows over it and it is gone, and its place remembers it no more. But from everlasting to everlasting the Lord's love is with those who fear him . . ." (Psalm 103:15-17 NIV).

If you are a Christian, no doubt you are well versed on God's eternal plan for you following your physical death. This morning, I want to share with you about death from a different perspective. Let's begin with these questions: If you were to die today, how would you be remembered? How do you want to be remembered by your family, friends, and acquaintances after you are gone? What would you like people to say about your life?

I think most of us would answer these questions something like this: "I would like to be remembered as a godly, kind, loving, caring, compassionate, and giving person—as a good parent who gave his best to his family, etc." I doubt any of us would say we want to be remembered by how much money we made, the size of the house in which we lived, or the kind of car we drove. Yet many of us are driven by a selfish desire for such material things in this life.

However, when we come face to face with the prospect of death, our values immediately take on a more wholesome and spiritual quality. How about those values while you live?

You must live today the way you want to be remembered. People's opinions of you are being formed today by what you say and do. Each of us would be wise to pause and think about how we would want to be remembered, then start working our way backwards to the present. Start doing those things now: loving, serving, giving, etc.

At the end of your life, what evidence will there have been that you were a Christian? Jesus said, *"By their fruit you will recognize them"* (Matthew 7:16 NIV). Here are some things that will determine how we are remembered, according to A. W. Tozer:

1. What we want most.
2. What we think most about.
3. How we use our money.
4. What we do with our leisure time.
5. The company we enjoy.
6. Who and what we admire.
7. What we laugh at.

Robert Morris said, *"I hate funerals and would not attend my own if it could be avoided, but it is well for every person to stop once in a while to think of what sort of a collection of mourners he is training for his final event."*

Sep 19

Chuckle: *"You know you're getting old when you bend over in the morning to tie your shoes and realize you didn't take them off the night before!"*

Quote: *"It is we ourselves and not outward circumstances who make death what it can be, a death freely and voluntarily accepted."* ~ Deitrich Bonhoeffer

Courage to Face Death

"For we are not our own masters when we live or when we die. While we live, we live to please the Lord. And when we die, we go to be with the Lord. So in life and in death, we belong to the Lord" (Romans 14:7 NLT). "Death is swallowed up in victory. Where, O death, is your victory? Where O death is your sting?" (1 Corinthians 15:54-55 NLT).

The Bible has much to say about death: its certainty, its meaning, and its defeat for the Christian. For those facing imminent death and suffering severe pain, death often becomes a welcomed relief. But most of us want to avoid death as long as possible. The will to survive has to be the strongest instinctive human trait.

As Christians, I think we are most afraid of the process of dying rather than death itself. We often talk about having no fear of death, but most of us want to live in this life as long as possible. Having said this, every one of us should be planning for the day our lives will end. Life is so terribly brief, fragile, and uncertain. We have no guarantee of tomorrow, much less next month or next year. *"What is your life? You are a mist that appears for a little while and then vanishes. Instead, you ought to say, 'If it is the Lord's will, we will live and do this or that'"* (James 4:14-15 NIV).

It takes faith and God-given courage to look death in the face and see it for what it is: the transition from this earthly physical life to our eternal life in God's presence in a place the Bible calls heaven. And the truth of God's Word is that when we know God through faith in Jesus Christ, we should not waste our time worrying about or dreading death. We should not be afraid. Instead, we should spend our time preparing for it. By His resurrection, Jesus was victorious over sin, death, and the grave.

How then can we have the courage to face our death without fear? It's really very simple—we must surrender our lives totally to Jesus Christ and trust Him completely in death as well as in life. As we claim His promises of our resurrection and eternal life, He will give us all the courage we need—even to face death. *"Even though I walk through the dark valley of death, I will not be afraid, for you are close beside me"* (Psalm 23:4 NLT).

"There are many instances of those whose faith has triumphed in the hour of death. D. L. Moody, the great evangelist of the past century, said on his deathbed, 'Earth is receding, heaven is approaching. This is my crowning day!'"

The reality of death casts a scary shadow over our lives because we are entirely helpless to prevent it. Death comes to each of us. *". . . it is appointed unto men once to die, but after this the judgment . . ."* (Hebrews 9:27 KJV). But there is One who promises to walk with us through death's dark valley and bring us safely to the other side.

Sep 20

Chuckle: Places to visit: *"I would like to go to Conclusions, but you have to jump to get there, and I'm not too much on physical activity anymore."*

Quote: *"Appreciation is thanking, recognition is seeing, and encouragement is bringing hope for the future."* ~ Anonymous

Stepping Stone or Stumbling Block

"Think of (consider) ways to encourage one another to outbursts of love and good deeds" (Hebrews 10:24 NLT).

I once read about an elderly lady who said: *"As a Christian, you can either be a stepping stone or a stumbling block. It's your choice."* As I thought about this passage and this woman's statement, I realized that at times, I have been both a stumbling block and a stepping stone to others. We are always being one or the other depending upon the choice we make at that moment.

"Think of" and *"consider"* are translations of a word that means a kind of rivalry. The thought may be translated, "let us rival one another as we stir up, spur, and encourage one another to love others and do good deeds for them." This is a kind of rivalry which is not contentious or bitter but both constructive and productive. It is a spiritual rivalry which causes us to utilize all our spiritual resources as we encourage and rival one another in love and acts of kindness.

Every day we make choices that influence the lives of those around us. Not making a choice is to choose to be a stumbling block—there is no neutral ground. We are either encouraging others by our words and actions or we are discouraging others by our words and actions. Just as Jesus said, *"He who is not with me is against me, and he who does not gather with me scatters."* We cannot be neutral. There is no such thing as Christian non-responsibility.

Think with me about your life. Do you know fellow believers who need a kind word, a pat on the back, or an understanding ear to listen? Have you chosen to be a stepping stone by spurring other Christians on toward greater faithfulness? When you choose to make a difference, you not only benefit your brothers and sisters but bring great joy to yourself as well. It's been my experience that a serving Christian is a happy Christian.

If we take the time to be sensitive to the needs of others, with the accompanying opportunities for service, we can be stepping stones. Being a stepping stone may be as simple as making a phone call, sending an e-mail, or posting a thoughtful card. Or it may mean making significant personal sacrifices of time, money, and effort to help and encourage other believers.

If we choose to do so, you and I can brighten the day of someone and be a stepping stone for our brothers and sisters in Christ.

Sep 21

Chuckle: *"My doctor told me to start my exercise program very gradually. So, today, I drove past a store that sells sweat pants."*

Quote: *"Faith consists in believing not what seems true, but what seems false to our understanding."* ~ Voltaire

From Facts to Faith

"This Good News tells us how God makes us right (righteous) in his sight. This is accomplished from start to finish by faith. As the Scriptures say, 'It is through faith that a righteous person has (eternal) life'" (Romans 1:17 NLT). *"The righteousness from God comes through faith in Jesus Christ to all who believe"* (Romans 3:22 NIV). *"So, you see, it is impossible to please God without faith"* (Hebrews 11:6a NLT).

My heart breaks when I see a person who just cannot (or will not) make the transition from believing the facts about Jesus Christ to placing his/her faith (trust) in Him as personal Lord and Savior. Many of these are good people, morally. The Scriptures, including many words from Jesus Himself, teach us to live clean moral lives as evidenced by integrity, compassion, kindness, and ministry to others. But is living a morally good life enough?

By both words and actions, many express their intellectual belief in the facts about Jesus and have adopted His moral teachings as the standard for their lives. In essence they say, "If I do my best to live a good life and treat others as I would like to be treated, then I will be right with God." Nothing could be further from the truth. This attitude begs the question: how good is good enough? Answer: None of us can ever be good enough to please God or earn the salvation of our eternal souls and gain entrance into heaven. Faith is the only way. *"For it is by grace you have been saved through faith—and this not from yourselves, it is a gift of God—not by works, so that no one can boast"* (Ephesians 2:8-9 NIV).

Trying to earn your salvation by any means except sincere faith in Jesus Christ is to proclaim yourself as God and as such, see yourself as fully capable of preparing for eternity in your own strength. Please don't let Satan entice you into adopting this mind-set. Instead, let the love of Christ draw you into placing your faith in Him and Him alone. If being good was the solution to our sin problem, why did Jesus need to die?

Please go back up to our Scripture passages and read them prayerfully with an open mind and allow God's Holy Spirit to give you the courage to begin living by faith every day. If you have not done so, pray to receive Jesus Christ into your life, trust Him as Savior and Lord, and commit your life to Him by serving Him. Then receive the joy which awaits you in Christ.

Sep 22

Chuckle: *"I wonder why people say 'amen' and not 'awomen'? Bobby asked.*

His little friend replied, "Because they sing 'hymns' and not 'hers,' silly?"

Quote: *"The danger of our becoming lukewarm is not from without—the danger is within."* ~ Reed Smoot

Lukewarm Christians

"I know your deeds, that you are neither cold or hot. I wish you were one or the other! So, because you are Lukewarm—neither hot nor cold—I am about to spit you out of my mouth" (Revelation 3:15-16 NIV).

Laodicea was a wealthy city that had always had a problem with its water supply. At one time an aqueduct brought water to the city from some hot springs. But by the time the water reached the city, it was neither hot nor refreshingly cool—only lukewarm. Because the Laodiceans had become lukewarm, they had become distasteful to the Lord—like a lukewarm drink. This metaphor describes a church that had become complacent and self-satisfied, and was destroying itself with the status-quo. They saw no need for change nor to be concerned.

There should be excitement, zeal, and fervor in everything we do for our Lord. *"Never be lacking in zeal, but keep your spiritual fervor, serving the Lord"* (Romans 12:11 NIV). However, the greatest sickness that plagues the church today is half-hearted complacency by its members. What constitutes a lukewarm-warm Christian?

<u>First</u>, lukewarm Christians are not those who stay home on Sundays without cause and make no pretense of living for

God. No, those are the "cold" ones. However, these seem to be more preferable to God than the lukewarm ones because they are not pretending to be something they are not. *"I wish you were (hot or cold) one or the other."* No, the "lukewarm" ones are the ones who may attend church, but give little of their attention, time, finances, and energy in worship or service to our Lord.

Second, to the lukewarm Christian, church has become little more than a ritual in their lives. They attend and go through the motions of worship—and feel they have fulfilled their religious duty for the week. They don't give much serious thought to spiritual matters again until the next time they take their Sunday clothes out of the closet. Their lives do not reflect active service for their Lord.

Third, the lukewarm Christian has a sense of contentment and peace about their Christianity. They are unaware of how far they are from where God wants them to be. Jesus said to the Laodiceans, *"You say, 'I am rich; I have acquired wealth and do not need a thing.' But you do not realize that you are wretched, pitiful, poor, blind and naked"* (Revelation 3:17 NIV).

Each of us has become "lukewarm" at some point in our Christian experience. However, God wants us to be happy, loving, excited, and active Christians deeply involved in the worship, fellowship and ministries of the local church.

Sep 23

Chuckle: *"Mama," asked the little girl, "if men go to heaven, too, why don't angels have whiskers?"*

"Because, dear," her mother answered, "men get to heaven by a very close shave." ~ Gertrude Pierson

Quote: *"Because of indifference, one dies before one actually dies."* ~ Elie Wiesel

Cure for Lukewarm Christians

"I know your deeds, that you are neither cold or hot. I wish you were one or the other! So, because you are Lukewarm —neither hot nor cold—I am about to spit you out of my mouth" (Revelation 3:15-16 NIV).

If, after yesterday's lesson, you find yourself "lukewarm" toward God and His church and you have been convicted by the Holy Spirit of your need to change, how would God have you go about it?

First, we must see ourselves as God sees us. If we have grown indifferent, comfortable, self-reliant, content, and without a burning spiritual purpose, we are lukewarm.

Second, we must have a sincere desire to change. This may be where you are right now. If so, please listen to these words from our Lord to the lukewarm Christians in the church of Laodicea. *"I counsel you to buy from me gold refined in the fire, so that you can become rich; and white clothes to wear, so you can cover your shameful nakedness; and salve to put on your eyes, so you can see. Those whom I love I rebuke and discipline. So be earnest, and repent. Here I am! I stand at the door and knock. If anyone hears my voice and opens the door, I will come in and eat (fellowship) with him, and he with me"* (Revelation 3:18-20 NIV).

Third, we must repent and allow God to change us. Let Him totally rework our attitudes and priorities. Listen to these words with an open heart! *"Never be lacking in zeal (lazy in your work), but keep your spiritual fervor (enthusiasm) in serving the Lord"* (Romans 12:11 NIV). *"Maintain your spiritual glow"* (Moffett). Also, the psalmist says, *"Zeal (passion) for your (God's) house consumes (burns within) me"* (Psalm 69:9 NIV). Repentance and cleansing are the keys to regaining that spiritual fervor. Our renewed zeal will result in the following (See Romans 12:12):

- We will be a joyful people. *"Be joyful in hope."*
- We will endure difficulties with patience. *"Be patient in affliction."*
- We will *"Be faithful in prayer."*
- We will serve others. *"Share with God's people who are in need."*
- We will *"Practice hospitality to everyone"* (Romans 12:12-13 NIV).
- We will seek opportunities for service. The body of Christ *"grows and builds itself up in love, as each part does its work"* (Ephesians 4:16 NIV).
- We will speak boldly about Jesus. *"For we cannot help speaking about what we have seen and heard"* (Acts 4:20 NIV).
- We will not neglect church attendance and fellowship. *"Forsake not the assembling of yourselves together"* (Hebrews 10:25 NIV).

God's kingdom, and this church, urgently need God's people to return to the "red-hot" zeal for Him and His work. We need spiritual revival! We need to get excited. We need to get back to the basics of being a contributing and happy Christian.

Sep 24

Chuckle: *"God put me on earth to accomplish a certain number of things. Right now I am so far behind, I will live forever."*

Quote: *"Man is never so tall as when he kneels before God—never so great as when he humbles himself before God. And the man who kneels to God can stand up to anything."* ~ Louis H. Evans

Praying in Jesus' Name

Jesus said, *"I am the way and the truth and the life. No one comes to the Father except through me"* (John 14:6 NIV).

For a Christian, praying should be as natural as breathing. In the same way that breathing is the body's physical response to the presence of air around us, so prayer should be the response of spiritual life to the presence of God's Spirit around us, in us, and with us. Prayer is our indispensable spiritual breath.

We talk a lot about prayer, and many attempt to pray. Some understand the secret to a powerful prayer that God will honor—others do not. Praying in Jesus' name is the only acceptable way for us to pray. Often when we come to the end of our prayer, we say something like, "I pray these things in the Name of Jesus, Amen." Do we really think about the meaning of these words, and their importance to our prayers?

If I'm not careful, I catch myself repeating these words at the end of my prayer without even thinking about them. I find myself saying them out of habit. In reality, they are the most important words we pray.

If we are serious about praying with power, we must learn: (1) what it means to pray in Jesus' name, (2) how to pray in Jesus' name, and (3) the results of praying in Jesus' name.

First: What does it mean to pray in Jesus' name? *"And I will do whatever you ask in my name, so that the Son may bring glory to the Father. You may ask me for anything in my name, and I will do it"* (John 14:13-14 NIV). Jesus said He would do whatever we ask in His name—thus validating His oneness with the Father. In this promise, does Jesus mean we have the right to ask anything our hearts desire, and be assured the request will be granted? The answer is "yes" and "no." We'll discover what I mean in our next two studies.

The name of Jesus is our authorization, or legal warrant, to enter into God's presence in prayer. As we saw in John 14:6, the only way for us to approach the Father is through Jesus. To have access to the throne of grace, there is no other way. Praying in His name gives legitimacy to our prayers and testifies as to the condition of our hearts.

When Jesus says we can ask for anything, we must remember that our asking must be in His name and consistent with His character and will. More on this subject next time.

Sep 25

Chuckle: *"The man who is forever criticizing his wife's judgment never seems to question her choice in a husband!!"*

Quote: *"Don't pray to escape trouble. Don't pray to be comfortable in your emotions. Pray to do the will of God in every situation. Nothing else is worth praying for."* ~ Samuel M. Shoemaker

How to Pray in Jesus' Name

"I am the vine; you are the branches. If a man remains in me and I in him, he will bear much fruit; apart from me you can do nothing. . . If you remain in me and my words remain in you, ask whatever you wish, and it will be given you. This is to my Father's glory, that you bear much fruit, showing yourselves to be my disciples" (John 15:7-8 NIV).

Last time we saw that it is only through Jesus that we have access to the Father (See John 14:6). We heard Jesus tell us that whatever we ask for in His name He would give it to us. I posed the question: "Does this mean we can ask anything our hearts desire in Jesus' name and God is obligated to grant our request?"

In our passage for today Jesus answers this question by laying out the conditions for praying/asking in His Name and having what we ask given to us. If we meet this condition, we can pray in Jesus' name with confidence that our requests will be granted. That condition: *"If you remain in me (joined to me) and my words remain in you."*

Just as branches are one with the vine/tree, in Jesus' analogy, God desires that we be one with Christ. If we remain in Him, we will realize that all our spiritual sustenance comes from Him through His Spirit within us. We will learn to depend upon Him and grow to (1) Understand the mind of Christ and think more like Him; (2) Understand His will, His ways, and His words; (3) Pray the will of the vine which Christ will honor; and (4) Ask only for that which is consistent with His character.

If we remain in Him and He is in us, we will pray in His name, ask unselfishly, listen to the Vine, and we will bear fruit. James 4:3 NIV says, *"When you ask, you do not receive because you ask with the wrong motives, that you may spend what you get on your (selfish) pleasures."* God will not grant requests contrary to His character (nature) or His will, and we cannot use His name as a magic formula to fulfill our selfish desires. If we are sincerely following God and seeking His will, then our requests will be in line with what He wants, and He will grant them.

Notice that Jesus said His granting our requests *"is to my Father's glory."* We bring glory to the Father when we pray according to His will. Because our hearts have been reconditioned by His Spirit, we can pray for anything we desire and we will receive. When we get to this point in our relationship with our Lord (the Vine), we will pray with complete faith.

Jesus said, *"Whatever you ask for in prayer, believe that you have received it and it will be yours"* (Mark 11:24 NIV). James says, *"But when he asks, he must believe and not doubt"* (James 1:6 NIV).

Sep 26

Chuckle: *Why is the person who invests all your money called a broker?*

Quote: *"Prayer is not merely an occasional impulse to which we respond when we are in trouble; prayer is a life attitude."* ~ Walter A. Mueller

Results of Praying in Jesus' Name

"I have told you this so that my joy may be in you and that your joy may be complete" (John 15:11 NIV). *"I tell you the truth, my Father will give you whatever you ask in my name. Until now you have not asked for anything in my name. Ask and you will receive, and your joy will be complete"* (John 16:23b-24 NIV).

In our last two studies, we have seen that praying in Jesus' name is the only way to gain access to the Father. Also, we saw that we must remain joined to Jesus and hide His words in our hearts if we are to expect to receive what we ask of God. We must pray according to the character and will of Jesus. Today, let's focus on how our lives will change if we pray this way.

We can readily see in our passages that our joy is of primary concern to our Lord. He shares the secrets of living in complete harmony and fellowship with Him, which will bring about this joy. He also says that when we sincerely pray in the name of Jesus, we will receive the desires of our hearts and our joy as Christians will be complete.

Previously people had approached God through priests as mediators. After Jesus resurrection, any believer could approach God directly. A new day has dawned and now all believers are priests (See 1 Peter 2:9), talking with God personally. That's why Jesus said His disciples had not asked anything in His name. When we pray in Jesus' name:

- Our joy will be complete—it is dependent upon exercising the privilege of prayer. Prayer is the spiritual life-sustaining breath to the believer. A praying Christian is a joyful and happy Christian.
- God's power will be evident in and through us. Someone has said, *"Prayer is the only omnipotence God grants us."*
- We will receive increased spiritual illumination. This new spiritual insight then allows us to increasingly pray in more perfect accord with His character and His will.

Our rewards for praying according to the will of the our Lord in Jesus' name will be answered prayers, sweet fellowship in His presence, and complete joy. The disciples no longer could rely on Jesus' physical presence for strength, comfort, and joy. The new experience of asking in the name of the ascended Christ brought them new power and new joy. Such power and joy remain available to all believers today.

Let me close with the words of Leonard Ravenhill. *"The church has many organizers, but few agonizers; many who pay, but few who pray; many resters, but few wrestlers; many who are enterprising, but few who are interceding. The secret of praying is praying in secret. A worldly Christian will stop praying and a praying Christian will stop worldliness. Tithers build a church, but tears will give it life. In the matter of effective praying, never have so many left so much to so few. Brothers and sisters, let us pray."*

Sep 27

Chuckle: *"After receiving the proofs of a portrait, a politician was very angry with the photographer. He stormed back to the photographer and arrived with these angry words: 'This picture does not do me justice!'*

The photographer replied, 'Sir, with a face like yours, you don't need justice, you need mercy!' "

Quote: *"Two works of mercy set a man free: forgive and you will be forgiven, and give and you will receive."*
~ St Augustine of Hippo

Mercy from God

"But because of his great love for us, God, who is rich in mercy, made us alive with Christ even when we were dead in transgressions. . ." (Ephesians 2:4-5 NIV).

Mercy is a special gift from God to each of us. In its simplest form, mercy is *not* receiving what one deserves. It is withholding the administration of harsh justice because of God's love and grace. There is nothing we can do to merit God's mercy; rather it is a product of God's loving and forgiving nature. Like grace, mercy is completely unearned and undeserved.

The story has been told of a mother who sought from Napoleon the pardon of her son. The emperor said it was the man's second offense, and justice demanded his death.

"I don't ask for justice," said the mother, "I plead for mercy."

"But," said the emperor, "he does not deserve mercy."

"Sir," cried the mother, "it would not be mercy if he deserved it, and mercy is all I ask."

"Well, then," said the emperor, "I will show mercy." And

her son was saved.

Mercy is the outward manifestation of pity and compassion. It assumes a need on the part of the one receiving mercy, and resources adequate to meet the need on the part of the one who shows mercy. God shows pity on us because of our sinful condition about which we can do nothing on our own, and He has provided a way of salvation through faith in Christ. Hebrews 4:16 tells us we should pray boldly for God's mercy: *"So let us come boldly to the throne of our gracious God. There we will receive his mercy, and we will find grace to help us when we need it."*

Often mercy and peace are found together in Scripture. When this happens, mercy is usually listed first. Mercy is the act of God, peace is the resulting experience in our hearts. Another way to define mercy is to feel sympathy with the misery of another person, and especially sympathy that is manifested by action to help that person.

"Suppose you see a brother or sister who needs food or clothing, and you say, 'Well, good-bye and God bless you; stay warm and eat well'—but you don't give that person any food or clothing. What good does that do? So you see, it isn't enough just to have faith. Faith that doesn't show itself by good deeds is no faith at all—it is dead and useless" (James 2:15-17 NLT).

Mercy is never deserved. If you find yourself having difficulty in granting forgiveness and mercy to others, please take a moment to reflect on God's mercy which has been granted to you.

Sep 28

Chuckle: *Mortal: "What is a million years like to you?"*
God: "Like one second.
Mortal: "What is a million dollars like to you?"
God: Like one penny.
Mortal: "Can I have a penny?"
God: "Just a second."

Quote: *"Costly grace is the treasure hidden in the field; for the sake of it a man will gladly go and sell all he has. It is costly because it costs man his life, and it is grace because it gives a man the only true life."* ~ Dietrich Bonhoeffer

Grace for the Humble

He (God) gives us more and more strength (grace) to stand against such evil desires. As the Scriptures say, "God sets himself against the proud, but he shows favor (grace) to the humble" (James 4:6 NLT).

If you are a parent or grandparent, your deepest desire is to give the best to your children and grandchildren. You want them to have everything they need to live healthy and productive lives. You want to instill in them the strength and humility necessary to face the trials and temptations that will surely come. The only things you ask in return is love, respect, and gratitude for what they have received. We want them to be thankful for what they have and unselfish when it comes to giving to others.

In a similar way, God wants to give us more and more grace and strength to help us combat the influences of the world, resist our evil desires, and live as His victorious children. God's amazing love for us is the reason for His amazing grace. As we humble ourselves before God, His grace freely flows to us without interruption. Grace is often defined as God's "unmerited favor." To put grace in perspective, remember that Justice is receiving what we deserve; mercy is not receiving what we deserve; but grace is receiving what we do not deserve. By humbling ourselves, we experience God's mercy and grace.

If a needy man rejected your one dollar gift, you might decide not to give him more. However, if he received the dollar with sincere gratitude, you would be more inclined to give him more. The dollar might be insufficient to meet his total need, but if refused, it would be sufficient to cut him off from further help. If we gratefully and humbly accept what grace God has given us, it opens the door for more and more grace to be given to us.

Pride makes us selfish and causes us to think we deserve all we can see, touch, or imagine. The result is greed and desire for much more than we need. God wants to release us from self-centeredness and the evil desires it brings, and to realize that what we really need is more and more of God's grace. This grace comes from a generous God when we honor Him and treat Him with reverence, love, and respect. To receive God's favor and grace, we need to humble ourselves before Him with gratitude. The remedy for evil desires begins with humility and ends with an outpouring of God's grace.

Sep 29

Chuckle: To her doctor: *"I have metal fillings in my teeth. My refrigerator magnets keep pulling me into the kitchen. That's why I can't lose weight."*

Quote: *"The commandment of absolute truthfulness is really only another name for the fullness of discipleship."* ~ Dietrich Bonhoeffer

Live in the Truth

"How happy I was to meet some of your children and find them living in the truth, just as we have been commanded by the Father" (2 John 4 NLT).

Have you thought about all of the places and circumstances in your life where you take truth for granted? When you slide your credit card, you expect truth to prevail and be charged the proper amount for your purchases. When you put fuel into your car, you expect it to be true that you're getting a full measure of gasoline as indicated on the pump. We expect the truth even when there is no easy way for us to verify the truth. As a society, we demand truth in advertising, transparent pricing information, accurate lists of ingredients, and demand compensation when our expectations are not met.

If we expect truth in our relationships, it should come as no surprise that God wants His children to walk and live in the truth of His Word. We should never intentionally distort God's truth either by our words or our actions. God's truth is eternal and never needs updating or revision. It is the same yesterday, today, and forever. Jesus said, *"Heaven and earth will pass away, but my words will never pass away"* (Matthew 24:35 NIV). *". . . , but the word of the Lord stands forever"* (1 Peter 1:25 NIV). *"Jesus Christ is the same yesterday and today and forever"*

(Hebrews 13:8 NIV).

An old music teacher picked up a hammer and struck a tuning fork; then said to his friend as the note sounded across the room; "That is A today, it was A five thousand years ago, and it will be A ten thousand years from now. The soprano upstairs sings off-key, the tenor across the hall flats on his high notes, and the piano downstairs is out of tune." He struck the note again and said, "But that is A, my friend, and that's the good news of the day."

In our passage, the apostle John expressed his delight in finding Christians following the truth of God's Word. They were members of the church to which he was writing. He went on to warn them against false teachers who were distorting the truth and discrediting Christianity. If we live with integrity, holiness, and a penchant for absolute truth as God defines it, we will be living in truth. *Jesus said, "if you hold to my teaching, you are really my disciples. Then you will know the truth, and the truth will set you free (from sin)... So if the Son sets you free, you will be free indeed"* (John 8:31-32, 36 NIV).

"Men turn this way and that in their search for new sources of comfort and inspiration, but the enduring truths are to be found in the word of God." ~ Queen Elizabeth, the Queen Mother

Sep 30

Chuckle: *"No true Southerner would ever assume that the car with the flashing turn signal is actually going to make a turn."*

Quote: *"If you think you can walk in holiness without keeping up perpetual fellowship with Christ, you have made a great mistake. If you would be holy, you must live close to Jesus."* ~ Charles Haddon Spurgeon

How to Be Holy

"As obedient children, do not conform to the evil desires you had when you lived in ignorance. But just as he who called you is holy, so be holy in all you do; for it is written: 'Be holy as I am Holy'" (1 Peter 1:14-16).

"Holy" is an often used word among Christians. What does it mean in practical terms for our lives, and how do we attain a state of holiness? In the simplest terms, the word "holy" means to cut or separate, it denotes apartness—set apart, and so the separation of a person from the common or profane life for a divine purpose. It also means pure or chaste. To be holy is to be set aside by God for His service and to be as nearly like Christ as possible. For unlike other creatures, man was made in the image of God and capable—through the power of the Holy Spirit—of reflecting the holiness of God.

When a Christian realizes who Christ is and what Christ has done for him through His grace, it tends to have a dramatic effect on his or her life, not only in salvation but in holiness." To be "holy" and to be "righteous" are quite similar terms. We are told in Scripture that we have no righteousness or holiness on our own, but any righteousness we might have comes from

Christ in us. *"There is no one righteous, not even one"* (Romans 3:11 NIV). *"But now a righteousness from God . . . comes through faith in Jesus Christ to all who believe"* (Romans 3:21-22 NIV).

C.S. Lewis once commented to an American friend, *"How little people know who think that holiness is dull. When one meets the real thing, . . . it is irresistible. If even ten percent of the world's population had it, would not the whole world be converted and happy before a year's end."* Howard Hendricks wisely observed, *"It is foolish to build a chicken coop on the foundation of a skyscraper."* The Christian who fails to live a holy life is failing to utilize the foundation for his life that Christ has given him. So we can say that to be holy is to be chosen, set apart, and strengthened by God's Holy Spirit to be like Christ. If we know Christ as Savior and Lord, His Holy Spirit lives within us to teach us, convict us, and to comfort us as Christ lives out His holiness and righteousness through us. This requires us to surrender every aspect of our lives to His control.

"But the day of the Lord (Jesus' return) will come like a thief. The heavens will disappear with a roar; the elements will be destroyed by fire, and the earth and everything in it will be laid bare. Since everything will be destroyed in this way, what kind of people ought you to be? You ought to live holy and godly lives as you look forward to the day of God and speed its coming" (2 Peter 3:10-11 NIV).

Oct 01

Chuckle: *Jonah's Mother: "That's a nice story. Now tell me where you've really been."*

Quote: *"Like farmers, we must learn that we can't sow and reap the same day."* ~ Unknown Source

Patience During Difficult Times

"Be patient, then, brothers, until the Lord's coming" (James 5:7 NIV).

Most of us don't like to wait in line at the grocery store, doctor's office, traffic light, restaurant, etc. Restaurants even have the audacity to call the attendants "waiters." After all, we're the waiters—we do all the waiting! We are an impatient generation and we want gratification right now, if not sooner.

Let's remember, "patience" is a fruit of the Spirit recorded in Galatians 5:22. To develop Godly patience requires the supernatural work of the Holy Spirit. In the next four lessons, we will be learning about patience.

As Christians, we need patience during difficult times. Those Christians to whom James wrote this first century letter were going through tough times—persecution, suffering, hardships. One meaning of the Greek word for patience is to wait with long suffering—never quitting even when the going gets tough. When tempted to throw in the towel and quit, stand firm and stick to it even when everything in you wants to give it up.

"Therefore, my dear brothers, stand firm. Let nothing move you. Always give yourselves fully to the work of the Lord, because you know that your labor in the Lord is not in vain" (1 Corinthians 15:58 NIV).

In a Christian's life, there are times of great emotional

joy—when God seems so close and so real, and your joy comes from serving Him. At other times, when it appears as if no one else cares about God or His work, you feel like the lone ranger, and are tempted to say "Oh, what's the use." James says that's when God will give you patience.

Extraordinary patience has been required of the Texas farmers during the recent extreme draught. Like that farmer who puts the seed in the ground and waits patiently for the harvest, that's what God wants us to do—plant the seed of the good news and be patient as God's Holy Spirit brings forth the harvest in His own time. *"You too, be patient and stand firm."* (James 5:8 NIV).

Oct 02

Chuckle: *"I have been in many places, but I've never been in Cahoots. Apparently, you can't go alone. You have to be with someone."*

Quote: *Hudson Taylor would tell those who wanted to be missionaries to China that there are three indispensable requirements for a missionary: Patience, Patience, and Patience.*

Patience Even When Rejected

"For examples of patience in suffering, dear brothers and sisters, look at the prophets who spoke in the name of the Lord" (James 5:10 NLT).

Like the prophets of old, we need patience when we face disapproval and rejection as Christians. The prophets persevered with patience even when they were laughed at, ridiculed, persecuted, or totally ignored. They stood up and spoke God's message whether it was popular or not without concern for themselves. They spoke whether people wanted to hear it or not. They showed patience as they waited on God to make things right.

Some of us may face ridicule and be otherwise mistreated because we know and love our Lord Jesus Christ. We need to be patient with those who treat us unfairly, and keep on loving them as Jesus loves them. The dictionary defines patience as: *"The capacity to accept, tolerate delay, trouble, or suffering without getting angry and upset."* The patient person takes a long time before he/she loses their cool and blows their top—even with the person at work who is always hateful and mean—that cruel kid at school—that cantankerous family member. Yes, we need to be patient and consider that their actions may be driven by some deep spiritual need.

No one treated Abraham Lincoln with more contempt than did Edwin Stanton, who denounced Lincoln's policies and called him demeaning names. Lincoln said nothing in reply. In fact, he made Stanton his war minister because Stanton was the best man for the job. Lincoln treated him with every courtesy. The years went by, and the night came when an assassin's bullet struck down Lincoln in the Ford's theatre. In a room off to the side where Lincoln's body was taken, stood Stanton that night. As he looked down on the silent, rugged face of the President, Stanton said through his tears, "There lies the greatest ruler of men the world has ever seen." Patience, love and understanding conquered in the end.

God's people are to be patient and love others as Jesus has loved us. Genuine love for people will go a long way toward defusing your impatience even when you face rejection and criticism. Just think for a moment about the love Jesus has shown you and the patience He has shown you even before you came to know Him as Savior and Lord.

Jesus said, *"Blessed are you when people insult you, persecute you and falsely say all kinds of evil against you because of me"* (Matthew 5:11 NIV).

Oct 03

Chuckle: *Sign in a Texas country store: "Be patient. None of us am perfect!"*

Quote: *"Patience is more than a virtue; it is a daily necessity. It is not an elective; it is a required course in the school of life."* ~ William Arthur Ward

Patience When Disaster Strikes

"Job is an example of a man who endured (disaster) patiently. From his experience we see how the Lord's plan finally ended in good, for he is full of tenderness and mercy" (James 5:11 NLT).

Personal disasters are perhaps the most difficult kind of trials for us to endure with patience, but there is no time when the need for patience is greater. I doubt if anyone in history has ever experienced such personal disasters as Job. In two days, Job lost his family (children killed in storm), lost all his possessions, lost his friends, and had a painful disease. His wife came to him and suggested he *"curse God, and die"* (Job 2:9c KJV).

God never told Job why he was suffering—why he was having to endure all those hardships. But even in face of total disaster, he continued steadfast in his faith. He hung in there. He never cursed God and never gave up. He said of God: *"Though he slay me, yet will I trust in him"* (Job 13:15 KJV).

Life's disasters come in many forms including financial ruin, painful loss of beloved family members, diagnosis of a terminal disease, devastating loss of house and other property during a natural disaster, etc. In times like these, the true metal of our faith is revealed. Each time I read the account of Job's extreme trials and disasters, I'm reminded that my disasters to date have been minor in comparison. Sometimes we see our relatively minor inconveniences and disappointments as disasters. Tornados, hurricanes, floods, earthquakes, etc., remind us that disasters can come at any time and when least expected.

When disaster strikes, our first reaction is to ask why a loving God allowed this to happen. As Job struggled to understand why these terrible things were happening to him, it became clear that God did not intend for him to know the reasons. He had to face life without satisfactory answers to the question "why?". It was only when he trusted God without answers that his faith became fully developed.

I think the operative question for each of us is this: Is our faith strong enough to remain unshaken no matter what disasters befall us? No doubt God allows our faith to be tested from time to time as He did with Job. When hardships come, can we progress from questioning God about "why" to hearing God's questions to us about our trust in Him? Can we stand the test with patience and say to God with Job: *"I take back everything I said, and I sit in dust and ashes to show my repentance"* (Job 42:6 NLT).

Oct 04

Chuckle: *There are many places I have never been, however, I have been in Sane. They don't have an airport; you have to be driven there. I have made several trips there, thanks to my friends, family and* work."

Quote: *"Though God takes the sun out of heaven, yet we must have patience."* ~ George Herbert

Patience When God Seems Far Away

"I can never escape from your spirit! I can never get away from your presence!" (Psalm 139:7 NLT). Jesus said, *"And I will ask the Father, and he will give you another Counselor (Holy Spirit), who will never leave you . . . he lives with you now and later will be in you"* (John 14:16, 18 NLT).

Our passages state an iron-clad take-to-the-bank truth— as Christians, God's Spirit is always with us and we can't get away from His presence. This is an amazing and reassuring truth for all believers. But if this truth is enduring, why do we sometimes feel like God is a million miles away? Good question. When things aren't going the way we want, we may feel God has abandoned us, is far away and is no longer acting in our best interest.

We need patience during those times when we don't hear anything or feel anything from God. In Job's case, all the things that were happening to him just didn't make sense. But they made perfect sense to God who was testing Job. Times like these come for all of us, and when they do, it may be that God is testing our faith. When we are willing to persevere with patience during such difficult times, then God will do a mighty work in our lives as He did in Job's.

If you believe you can never escape God's presence and

you believe the promise, *"never will I leave you; never will I forsake you"* (Hebrews 13:5 NIV), then God is never far away, but may be withholding evidence of His presence to accomplish His purpose in your life. *"And we know that in all things God works for the good of those who love him, who have been called according to his purpose"* (Romans 8:28 NIV). As He did for Job, God will bring good to you as He acts according to His will.

So, if you find yourself feeling like God is far away, draw near to Him by focusing your attention on Him in prayer, Bible study, and sincere worship. Then He promises to draw near to you (See James 4:8). If you feel that God is far away, that's all it is—a feeling. We must be patient and trust God's promises even if our feelings tell us something else.

Another thought: I was a pilot in the Army and learned early on that I could not trust my feelings when flying in the clouds with no visual reference to the ground. I had to trust the truth that the instruments were telling me about the airspeed, altitude and attitude of the aircraft. Trusting my feelings could lead to disaster, but trusting the instruments always brought me to a safe landing at my destination.

God will do that for you if you trust Him completely in all situations—including His promise to be with you always—rather than trusting your unreliable feeling that He is far away.

Oct 05

Chuckle: *"If at first you don't succeed, then skydiving is not for you!"*

Quote: *"The race is not always to the swift but to those who keep on running."* ~ Unknown Source

Winning the Race

". . . the Holy Spirit has told me in city after city that jail and suffering lie ahead. But my life is worth nothing unless I use it for doing the work assigned me by the Lord Jesus— the work of telling others the good news about God's wonderful kindness and grace" (Acts 20:23-24 NLT).

Have you ever considered your Christian life as a race? If so, are you content just to half-heartedly amble along and run with the pack? Or are you motivated to run hard, finish strong, and win the race by completing the mission God has given you?

I'm sure you have observed runners in marathons or other types of races covering great distances and have noticed the total dedication and exertion of the runners as they compete. The apostle Paul was prone to use such athletic events as analogies for being faithful to the task God has set before us as Christians. Even knowing the horrible things that lay ahead, Paul did not shrink from completing his mission. Drawing on this analogy, let's think about what is necessary to finish a race.

First, know the course the race will take—where you are going. Paul knew what he had to do and kept his focus on the finish line.

What marks the course we are to follow in the race of a Christian life? There are the five purposes of the church in which God wants us to be faithful: worship, fellowship, discipleship (becoming Christ-like), ministry (meeting needs of others), and evangelism (leading others to Christ). As you run the race, God will reveal His will and give you specific instructions in each of these areas.

Second, compelled by the Holy Spirit, persevere to the end no matter the cost. As the Spirit warned Paul that the way ahead would be difficult, He wants us to know the course will not always be easy and pleasant. Sometimes we feel like our lives are failures unless we are getting a lot of recognition, fun, money, success. But Paul considered his life as worth nothing, and unimportant, unless he used it for God's work. What is more important to you—what you get out of life, or what you put into it? When Jesus said, *"Take up your cross daily and follow me,"* He meant a life of sacrifice. He expects us to endure to the end, even when we "hit the wall," and think we can't go on.

Third, focus your attention on the finish line—winning the race. *"As for me, my . . . death is near. I have fought a good fight. I have finished the race, and I have remained faithful. And now the prize awaits me—the crown of righteousness that the Lord, the righteous Judge, will give me on that day of his return"* (2 Timothy 4:6-8 NLT).

Although you may not receive your share of earthly recognition, you will be rewarded by our Lord in heaven for your faithfulness during discouragement, persecution, or even death.

Oct 06

Chuckle: *Ben watched his dad build a pine bookshelf. "What are the holes for?" asked Ben.*

"They're knot holes," said his dad.

Ben asked, "What are they then if they're not holes?"

Quote: *"He that once sins, like him that slides on ice, Goes swiftly down the slippery way of vice: Though conscience checks him, yet those rubs gone o'er, He slides on smoothly and looks back no more. "*~ John Dryden

Living by the Spirit's Power

"So I say, live by the Spirit, and you will not gratify the desires of the sinful nature. For the sinful nature desires what is contrary to the Spirit, and the Spirit what is contrary to the sinful nature" (Galatians 5:16-17 NIV).

Sometimes godly parents have their hearts broken by wayward children who rebel against the spiritual, moral, and ethical standards they experienced and were taught in the home. When they left home for college, or to pursue a career, and were away from parental guidance, they fell under the influence of worldly company. They began to gratify the desires of their sinful nature which were contrary to what they had been taught.

Similarly, if we remain under the influence of our "Spiritual Parent"—the Holy Spirit—our lives will reflect the standards God sets for us. Jesus said, *"But the Counselor, the Holy Spirit, whom the Father will send in my name, will teach you all things and will remind you of everything I have said to you"* (John 14:26 NIV). But if we allow ourselves to move away from our Lord, we become indifferent to things of God. We then rebel against the Holy Spirit's influence and open the door for

Satan to lure us into gratifying our fleshly desires. We can easily fall into sin and out of fellowship with our Lord.

Our passage tells us that two major forces are at work in our lives: the cravings of our old sinful nature (evil inclinations and desires stemming from our bodies), and the power of the Holy Spirit within us. When you stop praying regularly, meditating on God's word, faithfully participating in worship services, and ministering to the needs of others, beware—Satan's enticement to satisfy the desires of your sinful nature has already taken root in your heart.

However, if you do not yield to temptation and consistently follow the leadership of the Holy Spirit, He will empower you to resist the cravings of your sinful nature and help you live by the Spirit's power.

Jesus said, *"Those who remain in me, and I (my Spirit) in them, will produce much fruit"* (John 15:5 NLT). Paul writes, *"When the Holy spirit controls our lives, he will produce this kind of fruit in us: love, joy, peace, patience, kindness, goodness, faithfulness, gentleness, and self-control"* (See Galatians 5 vs. 22-23 NLT).

Are these characteristics evident in your life? If so, you are controlled by the Holy Spirit. The Holy Spirit is by far the strongest of the two forces vying for control of our lives, but the choices we make determine which force will have control in this never-ending conflict within us.

Oct 07

Chuckle: *"I haven't spoken to my wife in 18 months. I don't like to interrupt her."* ~ Red Skelton

Quote: *"Prayer moves the hand which moves the world."* ~ John Aikman Wallace

Praying for Our Loved Ones

"It (this letter) is written to Timothy, my true child in the faith. May God our Father and Christ Jesus our Lord give you grace, mercy, and peace" (1 Timothy 1:2 NLT).

My wife, children, and grandchildren are so very precious to me that praying for them is as natural as breathing. Such prayers emanate from a heart filled with gratitude to God for sharing them with me and allowing me to enjoy the blessings they bring to my life.

I'm thankful for the privilege of approaching Almighty God, in the name of Jesus, on behalf of those I love. Scripture teaches us how to pray for those closest to us. Notice the three specific gifts that Paul requested for his beloved son in the faith, Timothy.

First, he prayed that *grace* would be extended to Timothy. God's grace is His unmerited favor, and the gifts He grants us reflect His abundant love and compassion for His own. In other words, grace is receiving what we do not deserve. It is through grace that God relates to us and allows us to experience His presence. God's grace brings us daily blessings even during difficult times. Most important, it is by God's grace through faith that we are saved (See Ephesians 2:8). But after we are saved, His grace blessings just keep on coming. *"The grace of our Lord was poured out on me abundantly, along with the faith and love that are in Christ*

Jesus" (1 Timothy 1:14 NIV).

Second, he prayed that Timothy would be granted *mercy*. Mercy is not receiving what we deserve. Each of us deserves punishment for our sins, but our merciful God, who wants everyone to be saved, provided His own Son to receive our punishment. *"The Lord is not slow in keeping his promise, as some understand slowness. He is patient with you, not wanting anyone to perish, but everyone to come to repentance"* (2 Peter 3:9 NIV). God, in His merciful patience, delays our punishment until we have had a chance to accept His gift of salvation. Nothing is more important than our praying that our loved ones will come to know Christ as Savior and Lord.

Third, he prayed that Timothy would be granted *peace*. Peace comes to us when we become confident that God's grace and mercy has been granted to us. Genuine peace will come when we claim the promise that His grace and mercy will give us sustenance even in the most troubling of times. *"And the peace of God, which transcends all understanding, will guard your hearts and minds in Christ Jesus"* (Philippians 4:7 NIV).

Jesus' words teach us the difference in His peace and the peace of the world. *"Peace I leave with you; my peace I give you. I do not give to you as the world gives. Do not let your hearts be troubled and do not be afraid"* (John 14:27 NIV). Henry Blackaby says, *"The world seeks to sedate us from the problems we face through counselling or drugs or temporary pleasures. The peace that God gives goes right to the soul, relieving the heart and mind."*

Like Paul, let's pray for grace, mercy and peace for our loved ones.

Oct 08

Chuckle: *"I always use notes when I preach, in case I say something I want to remember!"*

Quote: *"In God, we live every commonplace as well as the most exalted moment of our being. To trust in him when no need is pressing, when things seem to be going right of themselves, may be harder than when things seem to be going wrong."* ~ George MacDonald

A Work in Progress

"And I am sure that God, who began the good work within you, will continue his work until it is finally finished on that day when Jesus comes back again" (Philippians 1:6 NLT).

There have been times in my life when I felt I wasn't making much progress in my Christian growth and maturity. You may feel that way now or have felt that way in the past. Our lesson today, reminds us that each of us is a work in progress and that God will not be finished with us until His return or our lives on earth come to an end.

Our passage does not mean that your salvation is incomplete until Jesus comes. When a person first prays to receive Christ as Savior, he or she becomes what the Bible calls a "babe in Christ"—fully saved and destined for heaven, but that's just the beginning for a Christian. *"Like new-born babies, crave pure spiritual milk, so that by it you may grow up in your salvation, now that you have tasted that the Lord is good"* (1 Peter 2:2 NIV).

For a baby to grow physically, he or she is dependent upon proper food, exercise, instruction, and nurturing by his parents and others. Likewise, for a baby Christian to grow spiritually, he or she must receive spiritual nourishment from

God's Word, spiritual exercise through obedience to God, and many forms of nurturing by other Christians.

God will help you to grow in grace until He has completed His work in your life. However, you must have the desire and willingness to grow for God in order for Him to do everything He desires to do in your life. When you are discouraged at your perceived lack of progress in spiritual growth, remember that God will never give up on you. He promises to take you from where you are to where He wants you to be.

When you feel unfinished, incomplete, or distressed by your shortcomings, remember God's promise. Please don't make the mistake of letting your present condition rob you of the joy of knowing Christ or keeping you from growing closer to Him every day.

Someone said, "We have all been driving down a highway and noticed bright orange signs that state, 'BEGIN CONSTRUCTION' and 'END CONSTRUCTION.' Sometimes these signs remain around long after the construction work is over. If one of us were to announce—that for the time being—God's construction in our lives was going to be halted, would our friends say, 'I didn't know any construction was going on?'"

When God saves you, you belong to Him forever. However, once you are saved, God wants to continue His work in you until Jesus comes or the end of your earthly life.

Oct 09

Chuckle: *"Experience is a wonderful thing. It enables you to recognize a mistake when you make it again."*

Quote: *"You will rest from your vain fancies if you perform every act in life as though it were your last." ~ Marcus Aurelius*

A New Master

"Now get up and go into the city, and you will be told what you are to do" (Acts 9:6 NLT).

As I thought about these words of Jesus to Saul of Tarsus on the road to Damascus, I was reminded that we all serve a master of some sort. It may be greed, anger, addictions, lust, or anything else that controls our lives. Our master determines our actions, thoughts, and attitudes. What you think about constantly, spend a lot of time with, or expend resources on is likely to be your master. What, or whom, is your master? Before Saul met Jesus, his master was his unrelenting desire to persecute Christians.

As Saul travelled to Damascus in pursuit of Christians, he was confronted by the risen Christ and brought face to face with the truth of the Good News. You may not have such an encounter with Christ as Saul did, but every one of us who hears the gospel is brought face to face with the truth of the living Christ. And through the Holy Spirit, He speaks to us as He spoke to Saul.

These words of Jesus completely changed Saul's life. Until this point he had answered to the desires of his own heart and the traditions handed down from his fathers. But now he was to obey the voice of Jesus, the risen Lord, above all.

To receive Christ as Savior should include receiving Him

as Lord and Master of your life. Like Paul, Christ should be our new Master and we are to obey His voice above all. As we obey Him, we experience great joy—for He graciously leads us into God's perfect will. *"I take joy in doing your will, my God, for your instructions are written on my heart"* (Psalm 40:8 NLT).

After Jesus had changed his name from Saul to Paul, Paul refers to this conversion experience as the start of his new life in Christ. He saw the risen Christ and acknowledged Him as Lord, confessed his sin, surrendered his life to Christ, and resolved to obey him. Paul now had a new Master. If you have met Jesus Christ on your own Damascus road, and have received Him as Savior, perhaps you should ask yourself: "Is Jesus Christ really the Master of my life?" If Christ isn't the Master of your life, you would be wise to pray asking Him to teach you to put Him first, listen to His voice, and obey Him.

Maybe you are trying to serve two masters—God and something else that has control over your life. Jesus said, *"No one can serve two masters. Either he will hate the one and love the other, or he will be devoted to one and despise the other. You cannot serve both God and money"* (Matthew 6:24 NIV).

Jesus' words are especially applicable today. We live in a society where money and possessions are the masters of many.

Oct 10

Chuckle: He: *"I got this great new hearing aid."*

She: *"Are you wearing it now?"*

He: *"Yes. Cost me four thousand dollars, but it's top of the line."*

She: *"What kind is it?"*

He: *"Twelve Thirty."*

Quote: *"The blessed and inviting truth is that God is the most winsome of all beings and in our worship of Him we should find unspeakable pleasure."* ~ A. W. Tozer

Worship with Integrity

"These people honor me with their lips, but their hearts are far from me" (Mark 7:6 NIV).

Our Lord is not interested in ritualistic worship that does not come from a pure heart. When we worship, it should be a time of personal encounter with our Heavenly Father—a time when we pour out our hearts to Him in love, thanksgiving, and praise with an attitude of repentance and contrition for our sins. We should worship with excitement at the prospect of hearing God's voice as He speaks to us and directs us toward a more perfect relationship with Him. When we leave a worship service, our lives should be forever changed by what has happened there. It is impossible to sincerely enter God's presence in worship without being drawn closer to Him and becoming more like Jesus.

Hypocrisy is pretending to be something you are not. In our passage, Jesus called the Pharisees hypocrites because their worship was not genuine. They were not motivated by love in their worship but by a desire to attain profit, to appear to others as holy, and enhance their personal status. You may attend church because your spouse nagged you into going, or you may go in order to be seen and improve your image in your community while, at the same time, down deep in your heart, you would rather be somewhere else. When our hearts are right with our Lord, our motives for worship will be pure and our worship will be a result of genuine love for Christ and the excitement about the opportunity to let Him shape our lives. We will worship with integrity.

Luther Dorr shares about worshiping with integrity: *"The Lord brought home the need for me to worship with integrity in an experience I had as a faculty member of a Baptist Seminary. I had rushed to chapel services from the class I had been teaching. The first hymn was already being sung. I found the page in the hymnal and joined in the singing.*

However, my mind was still on some discussions we had in the class previous to chapel. I had sung three stanzas before I realized I had been singing the words from memory, not conscious of what I was singing, while my heart and mind were doing something else. I was participating in a worship activity, but I was not worshiping the Lord consciously through the words of the hymn. The Lord seemed to call me to get my whole self into chapel and to come to Him in worship with my mind and heart as well as with my physical presence and voice. I still have to do the same thing today."

Going through the motions of worship without a change of heart is useless in God's eyes. Above all, He wants a genuine love relationship with each of us. Because of this He gave us the Great Commandment, telling us to love Him with all our heart, soul, mind, and strength. God wants our worship to burst forth from our hearts out of love for Him.

Oct 11

Chuckle: *"The trouble with being a leader is that you can't be sure whether people are following you or chasing you!"*

Quote: *"Lord, for tomorrow and its needs, I do not pray; Keep me, my God, from the stain of sin, Just for today."* ~ Mary Xavier

Needs and Wants

"And this same God who takes care of me will supply all your needs from his glorious riches, which have been given to us in Christ Jesus" (Philippians 4:19 NLT).

We sometimes have difficulty distinguishing between our wants and our needs. As a society, we have become spoiled because of the abundant material blessings God has given us. As we read passages of Scripture about how God will supply our needs, we can drift into thinking that God should supply our wants as well. Expecting God to provide each and everything we desire shows a lack of understanding concerning God's promise to us. We may not always have all we want, but by trusting in our Lord, our attitudes and appetites can change from wanting everything in sight to accepting God's provision with sincere gratitude.

Jesus was teaching His followers not to worry about their basic needs like food, water, and clothing. Then He laid out a condition for God's meeting these basic needs. *"So do not worry, saying, 'What shall we eat?' or 'What shall we drink' or 'What shall we wear?' For the pagans run after those things, and your heavenly Father knows that you need them. But seek first his kingdom and his righteousness, and all these things will be given to you as well"* (Matt. 6:31-33 NIV).

God owns all things, knows all things, and sees all things. He is keenly aware of the needs in your life and mine. In fact, God often provides even before we become aware of our needs.

As a pastor, I have been amazed at the number of testimonies from people about God's goodness as He ministers to their needs. We can trust God in all areas of life. He will meet not only our physical needs, but emotional and spiritual needs as well. God even gave Paul the courage to face death. He will meet your need for comfort and peace when you lose a loved one. He will give you strength and peace to help you deal with a serious illness.

Paul's words: *"..for I have learned to be get along happily whether I have much or little. I know how to live on almost nothing or with everything. I have learned the secret of living in every situation, whether it is with a full stomach or empty, with plenty or little. For I can do everything with the help of Christ who gives me the strength I need"* (Philippians 4:11-13 NLT).

Notice that Paul had learned to be happy and content. Learning is a process of growing in faith. Have you learned to place God's kingdom and His righteousness first in your life? Have you learned to take God at His word about meeting your basic needs? Have you learned to be content and trust our Lord in every situation?

Oct 12

Chuckle: *"Why are buildings called buildings when they are finished? Shouldn't they be called builts?"*

Quote: *"Prayer doesn't get man's will done in heaven; it gets God's will done on earth."* ~ Ronald Dunn

Your Body: Temple of the Holy Spirit

"Or don't you know that your body is the temple of the Holy Spirit, who lives in you and was given to you by God? You do not belong to yourself. For God bought you with a high price. So you must honor God with your body" (1 Corinthians 6:19-20 NLT).

When Jesus found the money changers and merchants doing business in the temple, He became angry and forcefully drove them out. Then He said, *"The Scriptures declare, 'My Temple (house) will be called a place of prayer,' but you have turned it into a den of thieves"* (Matthew 21:13 NLT).

God condemns the desecration of His sacred and holy place of worship and prayer. The commercialism in God's house frustrated people's attempts to worship. It's no surprise that such actions angered Jesus. Any practice that hinders or interferes with genuine worship should be ended quickly if we are to please God. Let's look at our basic text which says our bodies are temples of the Holy Spirit.

Many think their bodies belong to them and they have the right to do with them whatever they wish. But under the guise of freedom, they become slaves to their own desires: sex, drugs, tobacco, gluttony, etc. You see, the Spirit of the Living God does not reside only in buildings, although He is there (omnipresent), but in the hearts of believers. Doesn't it track that our bodies, as temples of God's Spirit, should always be treated as holy, sacred, and instruments of worship and prayer? We should never abuse the temple of the Holy Spirit by mistreating our bodies. It is the Spirit within us that enables and helps us to live and pray in a way that honors and pleases God.

Now to our bodies as temples of prayer. *"And the Holy Spirit helps us in our distress. For we don't even know what we should pray for, nor how we should pray. But the Holy Spirit prays for us with groanings that cannot be expressed in words. And the Father who knows all hearts knows what the Spirit is saying, for the Spirit pleads for us believers in harmony with God's own will"* (Romans 8:26-27 NLT).

As a believer, God does not leave you alone to cope with life's problems. Even when you are at a loss for words in expressing the desires of your heart in prayer, the Spirit prays with and for you. Ask the Holy Spirit to intercede for you and help you to pray in harmony with God's will. Then, when you pray, trust that He will always do what is best.

Your body is the temple of the Holy Spirit who resides in you. You are not your own, but were purchased by God with the blood of Jesus. Your body should be an instrument of worship. And the Holy Spirit within you intercedes for you before the Father and helps you pray in harmony with his will.

Oct 13

Chuckle: *"Pharaoh's daughter was a great financier—she went down to the banks of the Nile and drew out a little prophet."*

Quote: *"Prayer is the contemplation of the facts of life from the highest point of view."* ~ Ralph Waldo Emerson

Prioritizing Your Prayers

"This, then, is how you should pray: 'Our Father in heaven, hallowed be your name, your kingdom come, your will be done on earth as it is in heaven. Give us today our daily bread. Forgive us our debts, as we also have forgiven our debtors. And lead us not into temptation, but deliver us from the evil one'" (Matthew 6:9-13 NIV). Some late manuscripts add: *"for yours is the kingdom and the power and the glory forever. Amen."*

The Lord's Prayer is quoted widely and has been beautifully set to music. It ranks with up there with John 3:16 as a beloved passage. These words from Jesus were meant to teach His disciples and us how to pray. Perhaps it is more accurate to call this the "Model Prayer." To me, John 17 is more appropriately called the "Lord's Prayer." But, as most do, we will call our passage the "Lord's Prayer."

When we pray, we are tempted to jump right in with our shopping list of personal requests for God to grant. But let's look at how Jesus prioritized the contents of this model prayer.

First, we take time to focus our prayer on God, not our requests. "*Our Father in heaven, hallowed be your name.*" In reverence and awe, we are to seek the face of God and express the content of our hearts in worship. By addressing God as our Father, we are acknowledging Him as not only majestic and holy, but as the very personal, caring, and loving God. We praise Him for who He is and for His loving relationship with us.

Second, we are concerned for God's universal spiritual kingdom. *"Your kingdom come."* In verse 33, Jesus said: "*But seek first his (God's) kingdom and his righteousness, and all these (material) things will be given to you as well.*" As we become concerned about the broader work of God's kingdom, our selfish desires fade into the background. Our concern for the kingdom also reveals our confidence that God will meet our needs.

Third, we desire God's will to be done, not ours, *"...your will be done on earth as it is in heaven."* We must resist the temptation to put our personal desires ahead of God's will for our lives. If we have adequately conditioned our hearts through worship, we can say with joy that God's will is paramount and we exchange our wills for His. We acknowledge that His will is best for us and we want His perfect will to be accomplished.

Fourth, we are then prepared to make our personal requests to God, including our physical needs as He wills. *"Give us today our daily bread."* We may think we provide for our physical needs ourselves by our ingenuity and hard work. But when we ask God for His provision, we acknowledge that He is our sustainer and provider. He wants us to ask even though *"your Father knows what you need before you ask him"* (vs. 8).

Oct 14

Chuckle: A child's comment on the Bible: *"Christians have only one spouse. This is called monotony."*

Quote: *"God has given us the freedom to withstand the Holy Spirit's activity in our lives. When we ignore, disobey, or reject what the Spirit is telling us, we quench His activity in us."* ~ Henry Blackaby

Spirit Controlled Life

"Don't be drunk with wine, because that will ruin your life. Instead, let the Holy Spirit fill and control your life" (Ephesians 5:18 NLT).

Here Paul contrasts getting drunk with wine, which produces a temporary feeling of "euphoria," to being filled with the Spirit, which produces lasting joy in a Spirit-controlled life. We should not be concerned about how much of the Holy Spirit we have but rather how much of us the Holy Spirit has.

As a branch subjects itself to the will of the tree, we should subject ourselves daily to the Spirit's control and draw constantly on His life-giving power to produce fruit in our lives. We have a choice every day we live: to be in control of our lives ourselves, or to be controlled by God's Holy Spirit. Which do you prefer? If we choose to allow the Spirit to fill us and control us, this choice involves two things.

First, it means saying "no" to self. There can only be one controller of the Christian life—Spirit or self. You must recognize that you are not your own. You are bought with a price—the blood of Jesus. You must dethrone "self." *"If anyone would come after me, he must deny himself and take up his cross daily and follow me"* (Luke 9:23 NIV). "In every person's heart there's a cross and a throne. You are on the throne until you put yourself on the cross. If you refuse the cross, you remain on the throne." ~ A.W. Tozer

Second, you must enthrone Jesus every day as the Lord of your life. When you really make Jesus your Lord, there is love, joy, peace, etc. These are the first fruits of the Spirit found in Galatians 5:22. This means that you have made Jesus Lord after His Holy Spirit awakened a need in you. This awakening is the work of the Spirit and it is He who gives you the desire to make Jesus Lord and allow His Spirit to fill and control your life.

To be filled with the Spirit is to be continually controlled by Him. The words in Ephesians 5:18 literally mean: *". . . . let the Holy Spirit continually fill and control you."* This means a daily walk with, and remaining in, Christ and continually being filled with the Spirit. This is what Jesus meant when He said, *"if you remain in me and I remain in you, you will bear much fruit."* Is He—at this very moment—controlling you?

There are two prerequisites to being filled with the Spirit.:

First, I must instantly confess my sin. The moment I become aware of a sin in my life, I confess it and receive forgiveness (1 John 1:9).

Second, I must practice immediate obedience to God. The moment God's Spirit impresses on me the need to minister, witness, pray, or whatever, I will obey.

These two practices will lead to continually being filled by the Spirit.

Oct 15

Chuckle: *"Middle age is when the broadness of the mind and narrowness of the waist change places!"*

Quote: *"I do not ask for mighty words To leave the crowd impressed; But grant that my life may ring so true My neighbor may be blessed."* ~ Unknown Author

Being a Good Neighbor Family

"Do not owe anyone anything, except to love one another, for the one who loves another has fulfilled the law" (Romans 13:8 HCSB). *"Love does no harm to a neighbor. . ."* (Romans 13:10 HCSB).

Christianity is a religion of relationships—a personal relationship with Jesus Christ and relationships with other people. One lady made this observation: *"I've watched Christian families over the years. One thing I have noticed is that they seem to be more interested in being at church day and night for meetings or services than in developing their family relationships. Why should I sacrifice my family in order to serve God?"*

Unfortunately, this observation has a ring of truth for some of us. It is our responsibility to model the Biblical Christian family for our neighbors and let them see the love of Christ demonstrated by the way we live day by day.

In this technological society, more and more communications are being conducted electronically and interpersonal exchanges and relationships are suffering as a result. Kids live on their cell phones, watching television, listening to their iPods, or playing video games. Families seem to spend less and less time together. Next door neighbors often do not know one another's names and never develop personal relationships. As Christians, our goal should be to model the life of Jesus. He sought one-on-one encounters with people of all walks of life and He taught us to love our families and to love our neighbors as we love ourselves.

How many of our neighbors see Christ being modeled in your life and mine? Because of our reluctance to build warm relationships with family and neighbors, how many are forced to observe our Christian life from a distance and form their opinions about Christianity based on those observations? To live out the sacrifice of worship is a Christian duty that extends beyond our church families to how we live as citizens, family members, and neighbors.

In our passage, Paul's emphasis is on the obligation of Christians to love others—an obligation that can never be paid in full since the law of love has no limits. This love should extend well beyond our own church families to non-Christian neighbors—the kind of self-sacrificing love produced only by God's Holy Spirit.

I encourage you to reflect on the quality of your relationships with others, beginning with your own family and nearby neighbors. Is your life one that draws others to Christ or pushes them away? Jesus socialized with sinners who considered Him a friend. How do your neighbors see you—as engaging or isolated? Do they know you up close, from a distance, or not at all?

Oct 16

Chuckle: *"Did you say that you fell over 50 feet but didn't hurt yourself?"*

"Yes, I was trying to get to the back of the bus."

Quote: *"It was a Person that God gave, it is a Person that we need, and it is a Person that we accept by faith."* ~ Walter Lewis Wilson

Jesus Is Always in the Boat

"A furious squall came up, and the waves broke over the boat, so that it was nearly swamped. Jesus was in the stern, sleeping on a cushion. The disciples woke him and said to him, 'Teacher, don't you care if we drown?'" (Mark 4:37-38 NIV).

Jesus and the disciples were together in a boat when a fierce storm came up. Think about the storms in your life—the situations that cause you great anxiety, fear, and maybe even panic. Through this account, Jesus taught His disciples—and us—a beautiful lesson about our faith during the storms of life. Here are four wonderful principles Jesus teaches us.

First: Even though Jesus was in the boat, the storm still came. This reminds me that even though Jesus is always with us in the form of His indwelling Spirit, storms will continue to rage in our lives. Jesus never promised that our lives would be free of troubles and trials. Just the opposite is true. He tells us we will encounter these difficult times, but He is ultimately in control and will give us strength to see us through them. Jesus said, *"In this world you will have trouble. But take Heart! I have overcome the world"* (John 16:33 NIV).

Second: Even though a storm was raging, Jesus still slept. During our storms of life, it's tempting sometimes to think that God is sleeping, has deserted us, or just doesn't care.

The disciples had seen Jesus perform many miracles and He had taught them much about faith and His kingdom. But, somehow their faith and trust in Him had become weaker, or non-existent, when faced with a difficult situation. Jesus says, *"And surely I will be with you always, even to the very end of the age"* (Matthew 28:20b NIV). *"Never will I leave you; never will I forsake you"* (Hebrews 13:5b NIV).

Third: Even though Jesus was present, the disciples were still terrified. Whatever your difficulty, you have two options: You can worry and assume that Jesus no longer cares; or you can resist fear, putting your trust in Him. When you feel like panicking, confess your need for God and then trust Him to take care of you. *"In God, whose word I praise, in God I trust; I will not be afraid. What can mortal men do to me?"* (Psalm 56:4 NIV).

Fourth: Even though they had little or no faith, Jesus still saved them." *Jesus got up, rebuked the wind and said to the waves, 'Quiet! Be still!' Then the wind died down and it was completely calm. He said to his disciples, 'Why are you so afraid? Do you still have no faith?'"* The beautiful lesson here is that, if we belong to Christ, He will never release us out of His tender love and care. Not only will He give us the strength and peace to deal with life's storms, but we have the assurance that ultimately we belong to Him and He has saved us for eternity.

Oct 17

Chuckle: *A Texas cowboy bought a Dachshund when someone told him to "get a long little dogie!"*

Quote: *"To worship is to quicken the conscience by the Holiness of God, To feed the mind with the truth of God, To purge the imagination by the Beauty of God, To devote the will to the purpose of God."* ~ Archbishop William Temple

A Life of Worship

"So here's what I want you to do, God helping you: Take your everyday, ordinary life— your sleeping, eating, going to work, and walking around life -- and place it before God as an offering (your spiritual act of worship)" (Romans 12:1 MSG).

When I mention the word "worship," what comes to your mind? For many of us, it would likely be Sunday morning services at our church where we are fed spiritually each week. That's a wonderful place to start, but that should not be the extent of our worship experience. We should worship God by offering to Him our bodies and everything we do.

I once read the weekly sermon in our local newspaper by Dr. Jeff Miller. He told the story of a mother who discouraged her children from feeding crackers to the seagulls along the beach. She reasoned that by feeding the gulls the children might destroy the birds' appetite for a more healthy lunch of fish. A fish market worker responded that the gulls received so much food from humans at meal times that they didn't fish anymore. They had lost their wild natural instinct to fish for their food. Dr. Miller went on: *"Just as the seagulls are dependent upon getting fed at a certain time of the day, I wonder if we are solely dependent upon Sundays to get spiritually fed."*

We see in our passage that everything we do every day

in life should be done as an act of worship. Participation in worship services is very important for our spiritual growth, but we certainly don't have to wait for Sunday morning worship services to be spiritually fed. If we take the initiative in seeking (foraging for) spiritual food, we will offer our bodies as living sacrifices and dedicate even the most routine activities of life to God as acts of worship. Because we hunger and thirst after God, we will regularly seek spiritual food from His Word. Then God will nourish us and cause us to grow in our faith through our everyday acts of worship.

God wants us to lay aside our own selfish desires and follow Him by putting all our abilities, energy, and other recourses at His disposal every moment of every day. He wants us to trust Him and depend upon His wisdom and guidance in every aspect of life. If we do this, worship will become a 24/7 activity and we will not become dependent solely on Sundays for our spiritual nourishment. Our actions on the job, in the classroom, or around the house will be done in a way that will honor and please God.

If we worship God during the week in all our activities, we will be much better prepared for corporate worship on Sundays.

Oct 18

Chuckle: *"People say that hard work never killed anybody, but on the other hand, I've never known anybody who rested themselves to death."*

Quote: *"The will of God never takes you to where the grace of God will not protect you."* ~ Unknown Source

Freedom from Slavery

"It is for freedom that Christ has set us free. Stand firm, then, and do not let yourselves be burdened again by a yoke of slavery" (Galatians 5:1 NIV).

A major hurdle we all have to clear is the one that says we have to earn our way into God's favor by doing good things for others and complying with a set of behavioral standards. The writer of our passage, the apostle Paul—formerly known as Saul—once persecuted the church and was zealous about keeping the Jewish Law and traditions because he believed he could earn God's favor through these activities. He tried his best to stamp out the early church because he felt God wanted him to do so.

Saul's persecution of the church may appear totally without justification to us. It's hard for us to understand how he could be so off-base in his understanding. However, when Saul met the crucified and risen Lord Jesus, he realized that favor with God comes through God's grace by faith in Christ alone, not in blind obedience to a set of rules.

"For it is by grace you have been saved, through faith—not by works, so that no one can boast" (Ephesians 2:8-9 NIV). Christ transformed Saul and gave him the name, "Paul" and sent him as a missionary to the gentile (non-Jewish) world. We can be

just as off-base as Saul was if we depend upon our being good to earn us salvation.

Through Christ we stand in God's favor—accepted, beloved, and free from the power and penalty of sin! Stand firm then in the freedom of God's favor today. Don't try to earn it but just stand in amazement and let your life show your gratitude for it.

The freedom God has given us through Christ is the freedom to serve Him, not freedom to do whatever we want, because that would lead us back into sin by making us slaves to our selfish desires. Some might say that freedom to serve Him doesn't sound much like freedom.

Listen to this illustration: Some years ago in Los Angeles a man was walking down the street with a sign on his shoulders. The front of it read, "I'M A SLAVE FOR CHRIST." The back of the sign read, "WHOSE SLAVE ARE YOU?" That's a good question, because all of us are slaves to one of two masters—sin or righteousness—Satan or God.

Let Paul put this freedom and slavery in perspective. *"But now that you have been set free from (slavery to) sin and have become slaves (servants) to God, the benefit you reap leads to holiness, and the result is eternal life. For the wages of sin is death, but the gift of God is eternal life in Christ Jesus our Lord"* (Romans 6:22-23 NIV).

Oct 19

Chuckle: *"You know it's going to be a bad day when your twin forgets your birthday!"*

Quote: *"We are the only Bible the careless world will read. We are the sinner's gospel. We are the scoffer's creed. We are the Lord's last message, Given in deed and word. What if the type is crooked? What if the print is blurred?* ~ Annie Johnson Flint

Eating with Tax Collectors

"That night Matthew invited Jesus and his disciples to be his dinner guests, along with his fellow tax collectors and many other notorious sinners. The Pharisees were indignant. "Why does your teacher eat with such scum?' they asked the disciples" (Matthew 9:10-11 NLT).

Tax collectors were among the most despised people in the Jewish society. They were seen as traitors because they collected exorbitant taxes for the hated Roman authorities who ruled over the Jewish people. The terms, "tax collectors and sinners" were used in the same breath. For Jesus to socialize with such people brought rebuke from religious leaders.

Undeterred, Jesus found Matthew—a tax collector—established a relationship with him, changed his life, and made him one of the Twelve. But the Pharisees were more concerned with their own appearance of holiness than with helping people. They showed their self-righteous attitude by criticizing of Jesus.

The longer we are active Christians, the fewer unsaved friends and acquaintances we are likely to have. We tend to become comfortable around those who share our Christian beliefs, values, and lifestyles. But if we follow Jesus' example, we will not be afraid to reach out in a friendly way to those who do not know Christ. We do this by getting out of our comfort zones and seeking opportunities to establish relationships with the unredeemed with the goal of leading them to Christ. Jesus' mission on earth was to reach out to those often shunned by "respectable" people. Following Jesus' example, we should share the good news with the poor, immoral, lonely, and outcast, not just the rich, popular, respectable, and powerful.

As we establish relationships with unsaved people, we must be careful that their lifestyles do not contaminate us. Listen to what God says in Jude 22 NLT: *"Show mercy to those whose faith is wavering. Rescue others by snatching them from the flames of judgment. There are still others to whom you need to show mercy, but be careful that you aren't contaminated by their sins."* As we reach out to the lost in friendship, we must be careful not to become so much like non-Christians that no one can tell who we are or what we believe. Lead others to Christ but don't let them influence you to sin.

This is what Jesus meant when He prayed for the disciples. *"My prayer is not that you take them out of the world but that you protect them from the evil one. They are not of the world, even as I am not of it"* (John 17:15-16 NIV). Like Jesus, we should relate to people who need to be saved, but we should not become like those we are trying to reach.

Oct 20

Chuckle: *As Shadrach said to Meshach and Abednego, "Is it just me or is it hot in here?"*

Quote: *"Righteous indignation is often nothing more than self-righteous irritation."* ~ William Arthur Ward

Judgment or Discernment

"Jesus said, 'Stop judging others, and you will not be judged. Stop criticizing others, or it will all come back on you. If you forgive others, you will be forgiven'" (Luke 6:37 NLT).

Because of our pride, it's so much easier to judge others than to deal with our own shortcomings. In dealing with this subject, we must understand the difference between being judgmental, and discerning right and wrong. Only God knows the hidden motives behind a person's actions and only He can decide if that person deserves to be punished. Ultimately, we, as Christians, will all be judged by Christ (See 2 Corinthians 5:10).

I believe a key motive behind Christ's warning against judging others is His knowledge that there's no way we can be judgmental and redemptive at the same time. After all, as Christians, we are God's ambassadors and His messengers to lead others to Christ. When you are judgmental, you are usually angry or bitter toward that person you are judging and criticizing.

If you find yourself with such a critical attitude toward someone, before judging try praying for that person. You will find praying for someone difficult, if not impossible, as long as your harbor your critical attitude. You will either stop praying for them or God will remove your critical judgmental attitude. If you continue to pray, you will find yourself loving that person rather than judging him or her. Jesus tells us we will be judged if we persist in judging others.

You may say, "OK, Jerry, I understand that I am not to judge others, but how do I deal with those I know are conducting themselves contrary to the standards set forth in God's Word?" This is a good and important question. It's answer deals with what the Scripture calls "spiritual discernment." Jesus tells us that we will know the spiritual condition of their hearts by the way they live—by the way they act—by the fruit they bear (See Matthew 7:16). It is the Holy Spirit who gives us spiritual discernment.

As we grow in spiritual wisdom, we become more and more adept at discerning between good and evil; between true and false; between the spiritual and secular. As believers, we are to observe the actions of others and discern whether or not they are pleasing to God, not so we can judge or criticize, but so we can, in love, help them become what God wants them to be.

God wants us to see others as He sees them. That is, we discern a person's sins while viewing that person through the filters of love and forgiveness.

Our goal should be to reconcile that person to Christ. *"And God has given us the task of reconciling people to him. For God was in Christ, reconciling the world to himself, no longer counting people's sins against them. This is the wonderful message he has given us to tell others. We are Christ's ambassadors, and God is using us to speak to you"* (2 Cor. 5: 18b-20a NLT).

Oct 21

Chuckle: *Golfer: "I'd move heaven and earth to break 100 on this course."*

Caddy: "Try heaven. You've already moved most of the earth."

Quote: *"A man that does not know how to be angry does not know how to be good."* ~ Henry Ward Beecher

Sinful Anger and Righteous Indignation

"My dear brothers, take note of this: Everyone should be quick to listen, slow to speak and slow to become angry, for man's anger does not bring about the righteous life that God desires" (James 1:19-20 NIV).

Wikipedia defines righteous indignation as *"a reactive emotion of anger over either an obvious or perceived mistreatment, insult, criticism, overpowerment, oppression, malice, etc. It is akin to what is called the sense of injustice."*

How can we be certain that our anger is righteous indignation and not sinful rage? I believe the answer is rather simple to state, but difficult to live out. Anger is righteous indignation when it is directed at that which angers Jesus Himself and when we react as Jesus reacted when He was angry.

Following Jesus' example, righteous anger and indignation are justified when we are confronted with sin and injustice. Some examples would be anger towards spousal abuse, child neglect/abuse, pornography, homosexual activity, racism, abortion, discrimination and the like. Jesus' anger and indignation, were directed at obvious sinful behavior and injustice. However, Jesus' anger was always couched in His overriding love and compassion. Even when hanging on the cross, He could have expressed anger and hatred toward His tormentors, but instead, He showed love and forgiveness by saying, *"Father, forgive them for they do not know what they are doing."*

When Jesus was angry with the Pharisees because of the hardness of their hearts, He did not exact revenge, but showed grief and compassion for them (See Mark 3:5). When we become angry, we best examine our motives before we act. We should resist the temptation to retaliate in kind or exact revenge when we, or others, are mistreated. Aren't you thankful that Jesus didn't react in kind to the rejections, insults and agony He suffered?

In McCosh's book, *Motive Powers*, he provides some cautions concerning righteous indignation.

"We may be angry and sin not; but this disposition may become sinful, and this in the highest degree. It is so when it is excessive, when it is rage, and makes us lose control of ourselves. It is so, and may become a vice, when it leads us to wish evil to those who have offended us. It is resentment when it prompts us to meet and repay evil by evil. It is vengeance when it impels us to crush those who have injured us. It is vindictiveness meant to give pain to those who have thwarted us. Then sin has already entered."

God knows our hearts and motives and we should never try to disguise hateful anger as righteous indignation. Destructive anger has a condemning component, while righteous indignation always has a redemptive component based on love and forgiveness. God provides us opportunities to channel our righteous anger into constructive ministries.

Oct 22

Chuckle: *"If you talk to God you are praying; if God talks to you, you have schizophrenia."* ~ Thomas Szasz

Quote: *"You realize there are a lot of amazing people out there to be grateful for . . . and a loving God, That's what life is about."* ~ Robin Williams

Remember, Then Thank God

"I thank my God upon every remembrance of you" (Philippians 1:3 KJV). *"Every time I think of you, I give thanks to my God"* (NLT).

A kind and thoughtful lady, who is a member of a church I once served as pastor, closes her e-mails by quoting our passage. There's something comforting and reassuring in knowing someone cares enough to think about you on a regular basis, and even more comforting that he or she prays for you and thanks God for you and your influence on their lives. Do you sense that you are fondly remembered by others with joy because of your acts of kindness and faithful service to our Lord?

Are there special people who have touched your life in the past that often come to mind and for whom you are deeply grateful? It might be that person who always knew when you needed a pat on the back, a comforting hug, a kind word of encouragement, or help with some other special need.

In this brief passage, we find two amazing abilities given to us by God our Creator that we often take for granted—the gifts of memory and gratitude. God gave us the ability to remember those who have loved us and contributed so much to our life experiences and to be grateful for them as blessings sent by God Himself. Perhaps you would like to join me today in remembering someone who has been a positive influence on your life in the past. Further, perhaps you will feel a desire to express your love and appreciation to that person using the words of Paul or similar expressions.

I'm sure the congregation in Philippi was encouraged by these words from the apostle Paul because of their love for him and his influence in starting their church—teaching them how to be fully devoted followers of Jesus Christ. Paul leaves no doubt how thankful he is for the faithful Christians in Philippi. He goes on to say: *"I always pray for you, and I make my requests with a heart full of joy because you have been my partners in spreading the Good News about Christ from the time you first heard it until now"* (Philippians 1:4-5 NLT).

Andrew Murray reminds us that "we think of Paul as a great missionary, the great preacher, the great writer, the great apostle. However, we do not sufficiently think of him as the (great) intercessor." Like Paul, we should be faithful in our prayers of intercession, especially for those we remember with extraordinary love and appreciation.

Oct 23

Chuckle: *A preacher related how he asked a group of high school students to write down their favorite hymns. One girl wrote, "Willie Smith."*

Quote: *"The way of the world is to praise dead saints and persecute the living ones."* ~ Unknown Source

Persecuted, Who Me?

"In fact, everyone who wants to live a godly life in Christ Jesus will be persecuted, while evil men and impostors will go from bad to worse deceiving and being deceived" (2 Timothy 3:12-13 NIV).

What is the greatest desire of your life? Our actions are driven by our desires and the perceived need to satisfy those desires. The operative question is what desires are we trying to satisfy? As a Christian, you know that God wants our greatest desire to be to love Him and "to live godly lives in Christ Jesus." If this is the greatest desire of your life, you will definitely find yourself swimming against the current in our culture, which is rapidly moving in the opposite direction. When our Christian values conflict with those of a culture that does not value godliness, we can be assured of a negative reaction.

A good measure of our desire to serve God is whether or not we are experiencing opposition. If we never find ourselves at odds with the worldly culture, then we should examine our hearts to see if we have lost our desire to serve God as our first priority. Jesus warned us about this when He said, *"Woe to you when all men speak well of you..."* (Luke 6:26 NIV). When the ungodly speaks highly of a Christian, it could mean the Christian has compromised his values to bring them in line with the prevailing culture. Sadness lies ahead for those who seek the approval of the crowd rather than God's approval.

The promise of persecution is not a pleasant one and it is not something we enjoy thinking about. Yet we need to be aware of the cost of godliness and be ready "to live a godly life in Christ Jesus" at any cost. Biblical truths should govern our lives, not the socially acceptable and politically correct values of our culture. Our ultimate goal should be to change our culture to once again accept God's standards and values.

"During the Watergate scandal, some people regarded it as a compliment to be on Nixon's 'enemies list.' They took it as a credit to them that people in the administration opposed them. In the same way, if you have enemies because of your righteousness, it will be a credit to you. You should be glad that you have that kind of enemies, and that they are persecuting you, because it means that you are not doing what they do. Instead you are doing what unrighteous men hate." ~ Illustrations for Biblical Preaching; Edited by Michael P. Green

Oct 24

Chuckle: *"An attorney specializing in personal injury decided to branch out, so he added libel claims to his practice. He wanted to add insult to injury."* ~ Sharon Berkey

Quote: *"When you go through deep waters and great trouble, I will be with you. . . For I am the Lord, your God"* (Isaiah 43:2-3 NLT).

Help for the Helpless

"The Lord is my helper, so I will not be afraid" (Hebrews 13:6 NLT).

Have you ever been in a situation when you felt totally helpless? Have you come to the point where no escape seemed possible unless there was direct intervention by God Himself?

This can happen to us on many levels, such as with health, relationship, or financial issues. Your circumstances right now may find you feeling trapped with no way out. Perhaps God has brought you to this point to help you realize your inability to move forward unless He helps by making a way.

Joshua had the Israelites camp by the Jordan River for three days before crossing it to claim the promised land. He had to make them realize their own helplessness. They were unable to move forward into that raging river and needed to acknowledge that it would take the hand of God Himself to calm it for crossing.(See Joshua 3).

Most times our feelings of helplessness come from issues within our own hearts. We begin to despair because our own solutions are inadequate for our problems, especially our biggest problem—the fact that our hearts are naturally set against God. There are patterns of sin and rebellion in our lives, and we feel helpless in the face of our own sinful tendencies.

Like the Israelites, it's only when we recognize our helplessness in the deepest level of our hearts that we begin to cry out to God, "Oh, Lord, I need the answer which only You can provide." *"But in my distress I cried out to the Lord; yes, I prayed to my God for help. He heard me from his sanctuary; my cry reached his ears"* (Psalm 18:6 NLT).

For God to do His greatest work in our lives, we must come to see ourselves as totally helpless and desperate. Helpless people are the most receptive to help. Self-sufficient people tend to struggle with life's problems in their own strength and refuse to seek God's help. But, when it comes to sin, we are all in the same boat. *"For all have sinned and fall short of the glory of God"* (Romans 3:23 NIV).

In our hopeless state of sin, God came to us in the form of His Son, Jesus Christ. It is in our helplessness that God's glory and the might of His power are displayed most. Only then will our lives make sense and we will begin to move against the current of our problems. We can go into any storm knowing that the Lord, the good Shepherd, brings calm and peace in the midst of our chaos. God does not always remove the problem, but He always walks with us and gives us strength to overcome it. *"God is our refuge and strength, always ready to help in times of trouble"* (Psalm 46:1 NLT).

God is not just a temporary retreat. He is our refuge and can provide strength in any circumstance.

Oct 25

Chuckle: *A man was showing his new clock to a friend. "This clock," he said, "will go for 14 days without winding."*

"Really?" replied his friend, "and how long will it go if you do wind it?"

Quote: *"Lose yourself in productive, creative and necessary work, and you will brighten, improve and enhance your own corner of the world. This is your responsibility, your privilege, and your calling."* ~ William Arthur Ward

Why Not Work?

"We were never lazy when we were with you. We never accepted food from anyone without paying for it. We worked hard day and night so that we would not be a burden to any of you . . ., we wanted to give you an example to follow. Even while we were with you, we gave you this rule: 'Whoever does not work shall not eat'" (2 Thessalonians 3:7b-10 NLT).

I want to preface this message by saying that we, as individual Christians, churches, other charitable organizations and society in general, have a God-given responsibility to care for those who are legitimately in need of assistance—financial or otherwise. We should never shirk caring for the sick, poor and needy (See Matthew 25:31-46).

Our beloved country was built by industrious people with a strong personal work ethic. Most of those in my dad's generation took great pride in their work and never wanted to be accused of being a slacker. They were reluctant to accept charity from anyone as long as they were physically able to earn their own way.

Even those who desperately needed help were often embarrassed by accepting it. They cherished their personal independence and worked hard to avoid being dependent upon others. Most would never seek personal gain through dishonest and fraudulent means.

Now, contrast the above with an all too common attitude today that says: "I deserve to be taken care of. I deserve what others have without having to work for it." Some even take pride in the fact that they can dishonestly manipulate the system to receive undeserved financial benefits. Sadly, the stigma formerly attached to dishonest gain no longer exists in the minds of many today. I once had a "Christian" neighbor ask me why I didn't dishonestly claim a disability to increase my tax-free retirement income.

In our passage, Paul advised the church to stop financial support to those who refused to work and persisted in their idleness. He was not advising the church to become cold, uncaring, and cruel to those with legitimate needs. No, just the opposite. However, he knew that idleness by the able-bodied could only be overcome when they learned to value work, not charity, for their livelihood.

The "something for nothing" attitude is all too pervasive in our society. As Christians, we need to set the example by reflecting unwavering integrity in every aspect of our lives—including our work habits. Like Paul, we should set an example for our family members and others with whom we interact. We must recognize that character and morality can never be legislated, and will only come through a change in values and attitudes.

Oct 26

Chuckle: *"Don't get annoyed if your neighbor plays his stereo loudly at two o'clock in the morning. Just call him at four and tell him how much you enjoyed it. . . .!!"*

Quote: *"Things that are holy are revealed only to men who are holy."* ~ Hippocrates

Take Time to Be Holy

"As obedient children, do not conform to the evil desires you had when you lived in ignorance. But just as he who called you is holy, so be holy in all you do; for it is written: 'Be holy, because I am holy'" (1 Peter 1:14-16 NIV).

One meaning of "holy" is *"to cut or separate. It denotes apartness, and so the separation of a person from the common or profane for a divine use."* In this context, God is the one that separates us from the world and designates us as holy and consecrated to Him. *". . . you are a chosen people. You are a kingdom of priests, God's holy nation, his very own possession. This is so you can show others the goodness of God, for he called you out of the darkness into his wonderful light"* (1 Peter 2:9 NLT).

God has set us apart as holy and belonging to Him and has given us a mission—to declare His goodness to others. When we accept Jesus Christ as Savior, we become members of His body—the church—and we are to join Him in His priestly work of reconciling people to God. We have been called to represent Him to others. *"We are therefore Christ's ambassadors, as though God were making his appeal through us"* (2 Corinthians 5:20 NIV).

The word "holy" also means being totally devoted and

dedicated to God in all we do. A holy person shows those spiritual, moral, and ethical qualities which God expects of those He has called and chosen as His people. Thus, God wants us to be holy as He is holy. As God's witnesses, we are to strive to live holy lives which will give credibility to our witness. As a reminder of what it means to live a holy life, please listen to, meditate on, and digest the words of this great old hymn, "Take Time to be Holy."

Take time to be holy, Speak oft with thy Lord; Abide in Him always, And feed on His Word; Make friends of God's children; Help those who are weak; Forgetting in nothing His blessing to seek.

Take time to be holy, The world rushes on; Spend much time in secret With Jesus alone—By looking to Jesus, Like Him thou shalt be; Thy friends in thy conduct His likeness shall see.

Take time to be holy, Let Him be thy guide, And run not before Him, Whatever betide; In joy or in sorrow, still follow thy Lord, And looking to Jesus, Still trust in His Word.

Take time to be holy, Be calm in thy soul; Each tho't and each motive Beneath His control; Thus led by His Spirit to fountains of love, Thou shalt be fitted For service above.

Oct 27

Chuckle: *In a very dark church building, a man said, "I make a motion we buy a chandelier."*

Another said, "I'm against it for three reasons: No one knows how to spell it to order it. There isn't anyone in the church who can play it. And third, we need more light in here!"

Quote: *"It is motive alone that gives character to the actions of men."* ~ Jean De La Bruyere

Motives Matter

". . . let your good deeds shine out for all to see, so that everyone will praise your heavenly Father" (Matthew 5:16 NLT). *"Take care! Don't do your good deeds publicly, to be admired (by other people) because then you will lose the reward from your Father in heaven"* (Matthew 6:1 NLT).

Our passage is from the lips of Jesus Himself as He delivered the Sermon on the Mount. In Matthew chapters 5, 6, and 7, Jesus teaches His followers the finer points of godly living. Here we discover that Jesus is more interested in the condition of our hearts than He is in our specific acts of kindness. He teaches us to do good deeds in ministry to others, but our motives for these good deeds determine their acceptance by God and our ultimate rewards in heaven.

Notice the apparent contradiction in our two Scripture verses. First, Jesus tells us to do good deeds for all to see. Then He tells us not to do acts of righteousness to be seen of people. But close study of Jesus' words reveals no contradiction at all. The differential factor is motive—why do we do good deeds. Do we do them to bring attention, honor, and glory to ourselves by the praise of other people, or do we do them to bring praise, honor, and glory to our Lord?

In our first verse, Jesus says our motive for our good deeds should be to cause people to praise our Father in heaven. In our second verse, Jesus warns us about doing good deeds to be seen by people to bring their praise to ourselves. Doing good to bring honor to God will result in His rewarding us for such service. On the other hand, if our motive for doing good is to bring glory to ourselves, we will not be rewarded by our heavenly Father. So, we see that motives really do matter to God because they reveal the condition of our hearts.

Satan will tempt us, in his sly and subtle ways, to pervert our motives for serving our Lord. We may have the purest intentions when we begin to do acts of kindness for others and honestly want them to bring glory to the Father. Then, low and behold, people begin to praise us for our actions and Satan tells us it's OK to bask in the warmth of that praise for what we have done. Then pride begins to raise its ugly head and our motives gradually change from bringing honor to God to bringing honor to ourselves.

This is what Jesus is warning us about. *"The Lord's searchlight penetrates the human spirit, exposing every hidden motive. God loathes the sacrifice of an evil person, especially when it is brought with ulterior motives"* (Proverbs 20:27; 21:27 NLT).

Oct 28

Chuckle: *"Warning notice at a seminary swimming pool: "First-year students are only allowed to walk on the shallow end."*

Quote: *"Freedom is what you do with what's been done to you."* ~ Jean-Paul Sartre

Freedom in Christ

"It is for freedom that Christ has set us free. Stand firm, then and do not let yourselves be burdened again by a yoke of slavery" (Galatians 5:1 NIV).

When we think of freedom, I hope we think of our relationship with Christ? However, many times we think of freedom as being released from some restriction which has prevented us from exercising our own free will. But, in the Biblical sense, freedom has a totally different meaning. Think about this illustration:

"Many people think that freedom is the license to do whatever a person wants, but true freedom is the ability to do what is right. It takes obedience in order to have true freedom. I can sit at a piano and be at liberty to play any keys that I want, but I don't have the freedom, because I can't play anything but noise. I have no freedom to play Bach, or even 'Chopsticks.' Why? Because it takes years of practice and obedience to lesson plans to be truly free at the piano. Then, and only then, does one have the freedom to play any piece of music. The same is true of freedom in living. To be truly free, we must have the power and ability to be obedient." ~ Illustrations for Biblical Preaching; Edited by Michael P. Green

As a Christian, *"you have been set free from sin, and have become slaves of righteousness"* (See Romans 6:18). Christ sets us free to enjoy the boundless gift of God's favor, but this freedom comes only with an obedient faith in our Lord Jesus Christ. Paul contends that we will always be slaves (servants) of something—either to sin or to righteousness. Before coming to Christ, we are slaves to sin. Afterwards, we should become slaves/servants of our Lord.

After we've been changed by the Holy Spirit, we no longer see freedom as doing our own thing but the will of the Father. *"If anyone is in Christ, he is a new creation; the old is gone and the new has come"* (2 Corinthians 5:17). As a child of the King, our whole concept of freedom changes.

In Scripture, we find two contrasting words to help us understand the biblical meaning of being free—grace and law. We have been set free from the Old Testament law and now live in the freedom of God's grace. We're not free to break God's laws, but our freedom and salvation are not earned by our obedience to laws. They are gifts of God's grace.

As Christians, we were saved from the penalty of sin when we accepted Christ as Savior; we are being saved from the power of sin over our lives; and we will be saved from the presence of sin when Jesus comes again. Our freedom is a call to be free from sin, and is the opposite of freedom to sin.

Finally, I'm reminded of the song, "Freedom isn't Free!" Of course, it refers to our personal freedoms that have been bought with the blood of our armed forces. But, our freedoms from sin are likewise not free. They cost our Lord everything when He gave His life for our freedom on the Cross. He shed His blood that we can be free! Free!

Oct 29

Chuckle: (church bulletin blooper): *"For those of you who have children and don't know it, we have a nursery downstairs."*

Quote: *"The death and resurrection of Christ is the heart of the Christian faith. Preaching Jesus as merely a good person who is an example of good living falls short of preaching the Gospel."*~ John Danforth

Grace or Goodness

"God saved you by his special favor (grace) when you believed (had faith). And you can't take credit for this: it is a gift from God. Salvation is not a reward for the good things we have done, so none of us can boast about it. For we are God's masterpiece. He has created us anew in Christ Jesus, so that we can do the good things he planned for us long ago" (Ephesians 2:8-10 NLT).

In his book, Faith and Politics, former Senator John Danforth uses the term "protestant liberalism" to describe a disturbing tendency in some Christian churches to preach and teach what I will call a "social gospel," which places major emphasis on living moral and ethical lives based on Jesus' teachings and example. Many of these same preachers seldom, if ever, bring listeners face to face with the stark reality of their sins and the eternal truth that repentance and faith in the atoning blood sacrifice of Jesus Christ is the only way to receive God's forgiveness, His free gift of salvation, and assurance of eternal life in heaven.

There is a place for such preaching and teaching, but not at the expense of the good news (gospel message) that God sent His Son to die on that cruel cross outside Jerusalem so that you and I can be redeemed, reconciled (made acceptable) to God.

We all know that Christians and non-Christians alike are capable of living moral lives and doing much for the good of humanity. However, the problem arises when people are misled to depend upon their good deeds to earn God's favor—trying to earn their way into heaven by being good.

Our passage clearly points out the sequence of experiences that result in salvation and then our doing the "good things" that God has planned for us to do. We are told that God *"created us anew"* when we accepted His gift of salvation through faith.

This tracks with another message: *"Therefore, if anyone is in Christ, he is a new creation; the old has gone, the new has come!"* (2 Corinthians 5:17 NIV). James also addresses this faith versus good deeds issue. *"But some will say, 'You have faith; I have deeds.' Show me your faith without deeds, and I will show you my faith by what I do"* (James 2:18 NIV). You see, we can say we have faith, but do nothing to show it; or we can do all sorts of good things without having faith. Neither approach will impress God.

Once we have a genuine salvation experience, our good deeds performed for the glory of God will bless the lives of people and ultimately result in our being rewarded at the Judgment Seat of Christ. *"For we must all stand before Christ to be judged. We will each receive whatever we deserve for the good or evil we have done in our (physical) bodies"* (2 Corinthians 5:10 NLT).

Oct 30

Chuckle: *Bob: Did you hear about the camper who was killed by a garter snake?*

Betty: That's impossible. A garter snake is not poisonous.

Bob: It doesn't have to be if it can make you jump off a cliff!

Quote: *"What God's Son has told me, take for true I do; Truth Himself speaks truly or there's nothing true."*
~ St Thomas Aquinas

Truth or Consequences

"Instead of believing what they knew was the truth about God, they deliberately chose to believe lies. So they worshiped the things God made but not the Creator himself, who is to be praised forever, Amen" (Romans 1:25 NLT). *"For the wages of sin is death, but the free gift of God is eternal life through Christ Jesus our Lord"* (Romans 6:23 NLT).

As I read our passages, I thought of a popular game show that aired from 1940 to 1988, first on radio then television. Contestants were required to tell the truth by answering impossible trivia questions in two seconds or suffer the consequences, which consisted of performing zany, hilarious, and embarrassing stunts. The show was "Truth or Consequences." In our passages, spiritual truth or consequences is laid out. It's not tell the truth, but rather believe the truth or suffer eternal consequences.

An amazing attribute of God is His granting to humankind the freedom to choose. People can choose to believe God and accept God's love and salvation through faith in Jesus Christ or they can refuse to believe God's truth and reject Him. When we choose not to believe, God will honor our choice and reluctantly allow us to muddle along in sin and suffer the eternal consequences of our unbelief separated from His presence in a place the Bible calls hell. It is the most terrible of human tragedies when a person deliberately and knowingly refuses to believe and rejects the truth.

The first chapter of Romans is a harsh indictment of people who suppress God's truth with their wickedness. Because of God's great love, mercy, and grace, He has revealed Himself in creation, His Holy Spirit, His written Word, and His one and only Son. *"For God so loved the world that he gave his one and only Son, that whoever believes in him shall not perish but have eternal life"* (John 3:16). The word "believes" in this verse means to trust in, have faith in, and commit one's life to Jesus. We are without excuse if we reject the truth.

Whenever we are confronted with a Biblical truth that contradicts, or does not reinforce, our own selfish personal beliefs, we will:

(1) Realize our error, accept the truth and allow God to change the way we think and live;

(2) Recognize the truth but deliberately choose not to believe it;

(3) See the truth as relatively unimportant and choose to ignore it; or

(4) Deem the truth to be archaic and no longer relevant in today's culture. Number (1) should always be our choice.

God's Word—the Bible—is the only reliable standard of truth, and we are wise to evaluate our beliefs in light of its teachings.

Oct 31

Chuckle: *"Some days you're the bug; some days you're the windshield."*

Good Thought: *"An obvious indication that we have not genuinely repented is that we make excuses for our sinful behavior."* ~ Henry Blackaby

The Need for Repentance

"For God can use sorrow in our lives to help us turn away from sin and seek salvation. We will never regret that kind of sorrow. But sorrow without repentance is the kind that results in death" (2 Corinthians 7:10 NLT).

"Noah's message from the steps of the Ark was not, 'Something good is going to happen to you!' Daniel was not put into the lion's den for telling the people, 'Possibility thinking will move mountains!' John the Baptist was not forced to preach in the wilderness and eventually be beheaded because he preached, 'Smile, God loves you!' Instead, the message of all these men of God was one word: 'Repent!'" ~ Illustrations for Biblical Preaching; Edited by Michael P. Green

Jesus Himself, along with Biblical writers, preached repentance as a necessary step in the forgiveness of sin and receiving eternal salvation. Repentance is a word that makes us feel uncomfortable because it requires us to change our ways of thinking and acting. The word "repent" means to change direction—stop going in one direction, do a 180 degree turn, and start going in the opposite direction. It means to be genuinely sorry and regretful for the sin in our lives. Repentance can be a life-changing experience.

Do you see repentance as a positive or a negative word? I hope you see it as positive and comforting. Just think about it! God, in His amazing love, has cared enough to warn us of coming danger and has given us the remedy for avoiding it.

Repentance is necessary if we are to be born again and receive salvation through faith in Christ. But the need to repent can also be a real problem for Christians as well. If you see repentance as a negative word, you will try all sorts of other actions in order to avoid repenting. Some of the ways we avoid being genuinely repentant include rededicating our lives to Christ; making resolutions to be more faithful to God; and being sorry for our sins, but unwilling to turn from them.

Repentance requires allowing God to do major surgery on your heart. It indicates a major and radical change in both heart and mind. It means we have come to see our sins as God sees them and we have come to agree with Him about their seriousness. Repentance requires us to take specific and decisive actions to bring our lives back into the center of God's will for us—to realign our thinking with His. Repentance requires us to change, not just have a desire to change.

In our passage, Paul warns about the dangers of having sorrow for our sins that falls short of genuine repentance. Being sorry we got caught, but not sorry for sinful action falls into this category. We can be sorry for the effects of our sins on ourselves and others but not for the sin itself. But a changed life will be the evidence that true repentance has occurred—the key to a victorious life in Christ.

Nov 01

Chuckle: *"Always keep your words soft and sweet, just in case you have to eat them."*

Quote: *"A truth that's told with bad intent Beats all the lies you can invent."* ~ William Blake

Truth That Wounds

"Out of the overflow of the heart the mouth speaks" (Matthew 12:34 NIV).

Careless and malicious use of the truth can be as devastating to others, and to our reputation and witness, as outright and intentional dishonesty, not to mention what it does to our spiritual life. Truth can be used as a weapon to hurt someone, and simply because something is true does not mean it should be revealed. Unnecessarily repeating a hurtful truth about someone can destroy their faith in people and cause them to withdraw from the church fellowship.

In our passage, Jesus says the words we use reveal the condition of our hearts, which is His primary concern. He is interested in what we say and do, but is more interested in the motives behind them. Before we say anything about someone, we should ask ourselves: Will my saying this be pleasing to God, and does it show love and kindness?

I have come across Christians who seem to get some sort of perverse pleasure from telling something negative about another person that, although true, can cause terrible pain.

Let's think about some ways that Satan can tempt us to misuse the truth in hurtful ways. A friend may tell you something about himself in confidence, but you find the temptation to share this information with someone else irresistible. You violate the confidence of a friend and used a truth to destroy a relationship, perhaps forever.

You may have witnessed the stumbling of a fellow Christian who has fallen into sin. As a fellow believer, what should be your attitude toward that person? As Jesus modeled forgiveness, kindness, and redemption for the woman caught in adultery, we should love and pray for that person and seek to help him/her repent of their sin and return to a Godly lifestyle. We should never shoot our wounded, but help them to heal.

Perhaps you pride yourself in "telling it like it is." But there's a huge difference in telling it like it is and being pure, holy, and edifying in our speech. Sometimes telling it like it is may not please God. We don't have to share that juicy morsel of gossip just because it turns out to be fact. Our words reveal who we really are deep down in our hearts. If we walk close to Christ, wholesome speech will be the fruit of that relationship. Words of kindness and hurtful words should never come from the same mouth. An untamed tongues reveals an impure heart. The heart of the problem is a problem of the heart.

Let's pray that God will give us hearts and minds modeled after Jesus and make a commitment to never use the truth to damage someone ever again. Being careful about what we say and how we say it is a sign of Christian maturity. *"Do not let any unwholesome talk come out of your mouths, but only what is helpful for building others up according to their needs, that it may benefit those who listen"* (Ephesians 4:29 NIV).

Nov 02

Chuckle: *"He charged nothing for his preaching, and it was worth it too."* ~ Mark Twain

Quote: *"I will study and get ready, and perhaps my chance will come."* ~ Abraham Lincoln

Preaching the Cross

"I know very well how foolish the message (preaching) of the cross sounds to those who are on the road to destruction. But we who are being saved recognize this message as the very power of God. As the Scripture says, 'I will destroy human wisdom and discard their most brilliant ideas" (1 Corinthians 1:18-19 NLT).

Unfortunately not all of us preachers are equally articulate and eloquent in proclaiming the gospel message. However, a lack of individual ability in preaching the Word of God does not diminish the importance and power of the message. The important thing for any preacher is that he speaks in the power of the Holy Spirit, not in the power of his eloquence. I urge you to listen to your pastor/preacher with a sincere desire to absorb the message and never with an attitude of a critic that nit-picks his delivery.

In verse 17 of our chapter, Paul says that God did not send him to give clever speeches/sermons with high sounding ideas, but to preach the Good News so that the cross of Jesus Christ would never lose its power. The word "preaching" means to evangelize or cast the net. The technical meaning is to proclaim good tidings. Here Paul is more interested in the content of his preaching than the method. The primary purpose of preaching is to bear witness and is the essential task of the Christian minister. But every Christian has the responsibility to proclaim the gospel message.

Please notice that the first letter to the Corinthian church is addressed *"To the church of God in Corinth, to those sanctified in Christ Jesus and called to be holy, together with those everywhere who call upon the name of our Lord Jesus Christ—their Lord and ours"* (1 Corinthians 1:2 NIV). Paul's words are for every Christian. You may not be a vocational preacher, but you certainly have a responsibility to proclaim the message of the cross.

Why is it so terribly important for each of us to be messengers of the "Good News?" It's because *"Salvation is found in no one else, for there is no other name under heaven given among men by which we must be saved"* (Acts 4:12 NIV). Each one of us who has experienced salvation through faith in Christ has a God-given responsibility, privilege, and commission to tell others the Good News.

You do not need to be a great speaker with an impressive vocabulary to share the Good News effectively. I believe the most powerful and effective way to communicate the power of the gospel is through your personal testimony of what Christ has done in your life. Many will respond to a simple testimony given with an attitude of love and understanding.

Nov 03

Chuckle: *A man to the meteorologist: "I thought you might like to know that I shoveled eighteen inches of partly cloudy from my sidewalk this morning."*

Quote: *"Let us endeavor so to live that when we come to die even the undertaker will be sorry."* ~ Mark Twain

God's Way or Man's Way

"Jesus turned to Peter and said, . . . 'You are seeing things merely from a human point of view, and not from God's'" (Matthew 16:23 NLT).

I remember talking with a precious grandmother who was heartbroken and worried because her grandson was making the wrong choices in life and was living by the ways of the world rather than God's ways. She could not understand why he had rejected her teachings and counsel on biblical standards of behavior.

To see the people you love ignore God's instructions and make dangerous and ungodly choices can bring much anxiety and heartache. This is especially true when you know they are headed for major disappointments as the result of their bad choices.

Jesus had just shared with His disciples that He would suffer, be killed, and would be raised on the third day. It must have concerned Jesus when even Simon Peter, one of Jesus' closest followers, began to evaluate what Jesus had said from a human point of view. Peter could not grasp the godly significance of what Jesus was saying and made the very human choice to correct Jesus by saying, *"Heaven forbid, Lord," This will never happen to you!"* (vs. 22).

Peter's words reflected a lack of understanding about the Father's plan for Jesus and for himself. It must have broken the heart of Jesus to find it necessary to rebuke Peter because of his inability to see things God's way. Jesus even addressed Peter as Satan, not because Peter was actually Satan, but because He knew the Evil One was influencing Peter's thinking and understanding. Peter *"did not have in mind the things of God, but the things of men"* (NIV). God said, *"For my thoughts are not your thoughts, neither are your ways my ways"* (Isaiah 55:8 NIV).

As parents, grandparents, or friends, we do not have the power to make choices for those we love. But we do have the responsibility to love them, lead them to Christ, teach them the things of God, pray for them, and help them understand God's ways and will as they make life's choices.

Each day we are wise if we evaluate ourselves to see if Godly wisdom is being applied in our own decision-making process. Are our decisions being made God's way or our way? Beware that Satan is always trying to get us to leave God out of the picture. Jesus rebuked Peter for this attitude.

Nov 04

Chuckle: Kid's comments on angels: *"Angels don't eat, but they drink milk from Holy Cows!!!" ~ Jack, age 6*

Quote: *"The trouble with opportunity is that it's always more recognizable going than coming."* ~ Unknown Source

Acknowledging Jesus Publicly

"If anyone acknowledges me publicly here on earth, I will openly acknowledge that person before my Father in heaven. But if anyone denies me here on earth, I will deny that person before my Father in heaven" (Matthew 10:32-33 NLT).

In many evangelical Christian churches, an invitation/commitment time occurs at the end of each worship service. This is to give people the opportunity to respond to God's appeal by making a public profession of their faith in Jesus Christ as Savior. Jesus does not intend that our relationship with Him be kept secret, but He requires a public acknowledgment of our allegiance to Him. During His earthly ministry, every person that Jesus called to follow Him was asked to do so publicly. Jesus expects us to let other people know we are Christians—followers of Christ.

This is a serious issue in a society where keeping our religious beliefs private is seen as desirable by some. Many do not think our Christianity should be acknowledged at work, school, or in any other public venue. There is a concerted effort by some to remove the very mention of God in all public government funded places. Yet we must understand what our Lord expects of us as Christians. When we share our faith one-on-one with others, we acknowledge our Lord in the most direct and fruitful way. Of course, as we acknowledge Christ before men, we must do so with the same love and compassion that Jesus displayed as He drew people to Himself.

We acknowledge our Lord by living according to God's holy standards and reflecting the love of Christ in everything we do and say. And acknowledging our Lord publicly by being His witnesses, brings His promises of eternal rewards. To receive rewards, however, should not be our primary motivation for being witnesses for Christ. We should do so out of obedience and heartfelt love and gratitude because of who He is and for what He has done for us—along with a great unconditional love for those who need to know Him as Savior and Lord.

"A Christian's life should stand out to the world as different. We should be like zebras among horses. When our lives are indistinguishable from the world's, we are like albino zebras. They really are zebras, their parents were zebras, they know they are zebras on the inside. But to all who see them from the outside they are no different from horses." ~ Illustrations for Biblical Preaching; Edited by Michael P. Green.

Jesus said, *"... let your light shine before men, that they may see your good deeds and praise your Father in heaven"* (Matthew 5:16 NIV).

Nov 05

Chuckle: A cop to a speeder: *"Warning! You want a warning? O.K., I'm warning you not to do that again or I'll give you another ticket."*

Quote: *"None but God can satisfy the longings of an immortal soul; that as the heart was made for Him, so only He can fill it."* ~ Richard C. Trench

Sympathetic God

"The Lord is like a father to his children, tender and compassionate to those who fear him. For he understands how weak we are: he knows we are only dust" (Psalm 103:13-14 NLT).

The term "sympathy" means the sharing of another person's feelings, as by feeling sorry for his suffering, or a feeling or condition that is the same as that of another. Please keep this definition in mind as we think about this attribute of our God.

A recurring truth of Scripture is that God is omniscient—all knowing. The very idea that God knows everything about us is both comforting and unnerving, depending upon our relationship with Him. God not only sees and understands what you are going through, He identifies with your trouble in a sympathizing way. If we come to understand that God knows, we have taken the first step in healing a broken life.

We are a fragile people, but God's care is unfailing and eternal. All too often we focus on God as a judge and law-giver while ignoring His compassion and concern for us. Each of us should be thankful that God's love, mercy, and grace takes everything about us into account as He deals with us. He will deal with you in a sympathetic and compassionate way, and you can trust Him in every circumstance. *"He (Jesus) felt great pity for the crowds that came, because their problems were so great and they didn't know where to go for help. They were like sheep without a shepherd"* (Matthew 9:36 NIV).

In this passage, Jesus showed His deep love and concern for people who desperately needed a Savior. The beautiful picture of God as the Good Shepherd is often used in Scripture. A shepherd dedicates his life to the care and protection of his sheep, and Jesus gave His very life so that each of us could be saved from the ravages of sin. His love, sympathy, and compassion come through clearly as you read the words of Jesus. He understands what you are going through because *"This High Priest (Jesus) of ours understands our weaknesses, for he faced all of the same temptations we do, yet he did not sin"* (Hebrews 4:15 NLT).

By dwelling among us here on earth and experiencing the same trials and temptations as we do, the God Man, Jesus, understands your life experiences and is there to help you through them by the power of His Spirit. By His example, He shows each of us that we do not have to give in and sin, even when we face Satan's most seductive lure of temptation.

Nov 06

Chuckle: A Child's Prayer: *"Dear God, we read that Thomas Edison made light. But in Sunday School they said you did it. So I bet he stoled your idea." ~ Donna*

Quote: *"To every man is given the power of choice."* ~ Unknown Source

Choosing the Important

"What good will it be for a man if he gains the whole world, yet forfeits his soul? Or what can a man give in exchange for his soul" (Matthew 16:26 NIV)? *"Do you not know that in a race all the runners run, but only one gets the prize (wins). Run in such a way to get (win) the prize"* (1 Corinthians 9:24 NIV).

The most important message I can relay to you from God's Word is to learn to choose what is really important in life. If we choose God's values, then we can have a victorious life. What's most important to you? Do you know? Let's make God's values our priority and align our lives with them. Let's think together about the importance of values.

First, living by Godly values reduces stress. A Gallup survey of baby boomers (born 1946-1964) asked what causes the most stress in their lives. The number one cause of stress was conflicting values. In other words, there was a huge gap between what people said their values were and the values actually reflected by the way they lived.

For example, most said family is very important to them, but the average father spent only five minutes a day talking with each of his children. Work, recreation, and other pursuits took first place in importance. Many said health is very important, but in the survey, many were overweight and didn't exercise. Materialism is bad and yet they spend all they make on "stuff." Many said God was number one, but when asked, "is God number one in your time and your finances?" most said "no."

Stress comes when you say, "I know what's important," but don't live that way. Such conflict in values brings anxiety, guilt, and frustration. James tells us that such a person *"is a double-minded person, unstable in all he does"* (1:18 NIV). We're pulled by competing values (God's and the world's). If we know the right values and bring our lives into line with them, then we can enjoy life without an unhealthy level of stress.

Second, your success is influenced by values. Values determine the choices you make and everything you do. Proverbs 4:23 NIV reminds us, *"Above all else, guard your heart (affections), for it is the wellspring of life."* Living by God's values will help you make the right choices, and with your success will come a sense of peace, joy, and fulfillment.

Third, and most important, your values affect your eternal salvation. You may be financially well off, but you may be spiritually bankrupt. Pleasure and possessions can become our gods and, if so, we miss the true God and His saving grace.

That's why Jesus warned *"What good will it be for a man if he gains the whole world and forfeits his own soul; or what can a man give in exchange for his soul?"* For what are you giving your life? Are you living to win the *"Crown of Righteousness, which the Lord, the righteous Judge, will award to me (you) on that day"* (2 Timothy 4:8 NIV)?

Nov 07

Chuckle: *"A mother found her young sons playing with a litter of baby skunks. Remembering a smelly experience she'd had with one when she was a child, she shouted out, 'Run, children, run!' Each boy grabbed a skunk and ran!!!"*

Quote: *"We make a living by what we get, but we make a life by what we give."* ~ Winston Churchill

Running with Skunks

"As God said: Therefore, come out from them and separate yourselves from them, says the Lord. Don't touch their filthy things, and I will welcome you" (2 Corinthians 6:16-17 NLT).

"When Jesus calls us out of the world, he doesn't invite us to bring our smelly way of life with us. But many church members still come to church every Sunday smelling like a skunk. The proof of Christianity is not a great church attendance record or a baptismal certificate, but a changed life. Following the Lord includes giving up unsavory friends and habits. And if we're really converted (saved), that choice isn't hard to make. When Jesus calls us, we have to leave our sinful ways behind. We can't follow him if we're running with skunks." (This quote is from an article by Doug Fincher, San Augustine, Texas).

It's true that after we become believers, God wants us to come out from among the sinful elements of the world. We have been set apart by God to take on the image of Jesus Christ. He doesn't want us to act like the world, look like the world, be like the world, or have loyalty to the world. But He does want us to remain in the world as a positive influence for Him.

In John 17:15, Jesus prayed to the Father for His disciples and all believers—including you and me—as follows: *"My prayer is not that you take them out of the world but that you protect them from the evil one. They are not of the world, even as I am not of it (the world)."*

It is God's plan that we be in the world but not of the world. To allow God's plan for your life to unfold, your allegiance and devotion must remain centered in your Lord while being used of Him to touch the lives of desperate people around you. You can do this by consistently avoiding even the "smell" of the world as a part of your life. The world follows Satan's agenda, and Satan is the avowed enemy of Jesus and His people.

As a Christian, the strength to remain free of worldly influence on your life comes from the Holy Spirit who resides within you. Just surrender your will completely to His and let Him have complete control. We can never separate ourselves completely from sinful influences. However, God wants us to resist becoming tainted by the sin around us while, in the power of the Spirit, never giving in to sin or giving up on the sinner.

"Show mercy to those whose faith is wavering. Rescue others by snatching them from the flames of judgment. Show mercy to still others,] but do so with great caution, hating the sins that contaminate their lives [] (Jude 22-23 NLT).

Nov 08

Chuckle: *TEACHER: "John, why are you doing your multiplications on the floor?"*

JOHN: "Because you told me to do them without using tables!"

Quote: *"Faith has no merit where human reason supplies the truth."* ~ St Gregory the Great

Faith Is Revealed by Actions

"Was not our ancestor Abraham considered righteous for what he did when he offered his son Isaac on the altar? You see that his faith and his actions were working together, and his faith was made complete by what he did . . . In the same way, was not even Rahab the prostitute considered righteous for what she did when she gave lodging to the spies and sent them off in a different direction?" (James 2:21-22, 25 NIV).

In summarizing his teachings on faith and works, James gives two examples of genuine faith from the lives of Abraham and Rahab. These two were so very different: Abraham was a man, Rahab a woman—a patriarch, a prostitute—a major Old Testament character, a minor character—a Jew, a gentile. They had one thing in common—real life-changing faith. Abraham believed God and followed Him. He put his total faith in God, and God made him righteous. He understood that faith is taking God at His word and obeying Him.

Rahab lived in Jericho, a pagan city—the first walled city the Israelites must defeat to claim the promised land. The Israelites sent spies to get the lay of the land and evaluate the defenses. When they got there, they stayed in Rahab's house and told her about God. She believed and put her faith into actions by hiding them, thus putting her life at risk. Abraham and Rahab are listed in Hebrews 11 among the great heroes of faith.

There are four basic truths about real faith. It:

1. is consistent with God's word;
2. is always centered on Christ alone, the object of our faith;
3. always involves the mind, emotions, and will; and
4. always results in good works (deeds). Jesus referred to these acts of kindness to others as "bearing fruit." *"By their fruits you will recognize them"* (Matthew 7:16 NIV).

For us to have the maximum impact on the world for our Lord, our faith and actions must be consistent. *"They claim to know God, but by their actions they deny Him"* (Titus 1:16). Ephesians 2:8-10 puts faith and deeds in perspective: *"For it is by grace you have been saved, through faith—and this not from yourselves, it is the gift of God—not of works, so that no one can boast. For we are God's workmanship, created in Christ Jesus to do good works, which God prepared in advance for us to do."* We are saved first by faith and then as God's new creation (workmanship), we are to do the good works that God has planned for each of us to do.

Finally, good deeds/works can never earn salvation. However, true faith always results in a changed life that produces good deeds. The true joy of being a Christian comes from the assurance that we have eternal life through faith in Christ, from obedient service to our Lord, and benevolent deeds of kindness and love to others.

Nov 09

Chuckle: *A patient told her doctor she had an episode of hallucinations. The doctor asked what they looked like. "Well, doctor, I really don't know," she said. "I wasn't wearing my glasses at the time."*

Quote: *"It is more important to maintain integrity than to amass a fortune."* ~ William Arthur Ward

Lawsuits and Christians

"When you have something against another Christian, why do you file a lawsuit and ask a secular court to decide the matter, instead of taking it to another Christian to decide who is right? I am saying this to shame you. Isn't there someone in all the church who is wise enough to decide these arguments? But instead one Christian sues another—right in front of unbelievers. To have such lawsuits is a real defeat for you" (1 Corinthians 6:1, 5-6 NLT).

Should Christians go to court against one another? Perhaps this question has never crossed the minds of most believers, but it deserves our careful and prayerful consideration. We live in a society obsessed with lawsuits. People sue each other over the most insignificant and ridiculous matters. It must be the "something for nothing" mentality that somehow being wronged even a little entitles a person to a windfall without working for it.

Obviously, lawsuits are justified in some circumstances, but as we study this lesson together, please remember the conduct of Christians should be different from the secular world. Our lives should give testimony that God has made us "*a new creation*" in Christ. We should have a different world view.

Here, Paul teaches how we should handle problems between Christians. We should not have to go to a secular court to resolve our differences. We have the wisdom of God's Word and His Holy Spirit, so why go to those who lack God's wisdom to resolve our differences? In love, we should be able to resolve disputes among ourselves.

Here are a few reasons why Christians should not take their differences to secular courts: (1) The judge and jury may not be sensitive to Christian values; (2) The reason for going to court is often revenge, and this should never be a Christian's motive; (3) Lawsuits between Christians harm the cause of Christ and cast the church in a bad light; and (4) Our love for each other should prevent our differences from rising to the level of anger, bitterness, revenge, or retribution.

"Be humble and gentle. Be patient with each other, making allowances for each other's faults because of your love. Always keep yourselves united in the Holy Spirit, and bind yourselves together with peace" (Ephesians 4:2-3 NLT). If we have this kind of relationship with one another as Christians, I don't think we will resort to lawsuits in most circumstances. Do you? It's true that some things must be settled in civil courts, but the bottom line for Christians is that we should take every precaution to avoid using them. By settling our differences in love, kindness, and understanding we send an important message to the world about the miracle God has performed in our hearts.

Nov 10

Chuckle: *Driving along I-90, just west of Chicago, I passed a sign posted by the police department: "Report drivers using a cell phone. Please call *99."* ~ Lane Martin

Quote: *"Have courage for the great sorrows of life and patience for the small ones. And when you have finished your daily task, go to sleep in peace. God is awake!"* ~ Victor Hugo

Pray Rather Than Worry

"Do not worry (be anxious) about anything; instead, pray about everything. Tell God what you need and thank him for all he has done. If you do this, you will experience God's peace which is far more wonderful than the human mind can understand. His peace will guard your hearts and minds as you live in Christ Jesus" (Philippians 4:6-7 NLT).

"A doctor had to give a painful shot to a four-year-old girl. When she learned what the doctor was about to do, her face showed her anxiety and her body tensed. As the doctor picked up what looked to the little girl to be a needle large enough to kill an elephant, she turned her eyes to her father, who then took her hand and fixed his eyes on hers. An expression of confidence and calmness came on her face. She knew she was not alone and found comfort, not in her father's spoken answer, but in his presence with her in her time of trial." ~ *Illustrations for Biblical Preaching*; Edited by Michael P. Green

Just imagine never worrying or being anxious about anything ever again! We are tempted to say this is an impossibility. All of us have worries and anxieties in our professional life, our homes, at school, etc. God understands our tendencies to worry and fret, but Paul tells us to turn our worries into prayers. If you want to worry less, then pray more.

I believe God intends for worry and prayer to be mutually exclusive. Maybe you are anxious about a financial matter, the health of your child, a rebellious child, your own health, etc. Any situation in life which we see as threatening to our peace and contentment can bring on anxiety. Some people even suffer from panic attacks brought on by extreme anxiety, worry, fear, etc.

In His Sermon on the Mount, Jesus says to us, *"So don't worry about everyday life—whether you have enough food, drink, and clothes. Doesn't life consist of more than food and clothing? . . . Can all your worries add a single moment to your life? Of course not"* (Matthew 6:25, 27 NLT). Here, Jesus is telling us He is aware of everything we need and promises to meet our needs.

According to Dr. Edward Poldosky, to worry is to deny the power of God in our lives. God's Word gives us assurance that He will care for us and meet our every need. When we fail to live by this promise, worry and anxiety creep into our lives and destroy our peace of mind.

God's peace is much different from the worlds peace. Jesus said, *"I am leaving you with a gift—peace of mind and heart. And the peace I give isn't like the peace the world gives. So don't be troubled or afraid"* (John 14:27 NLT). True God-given peace comes from knowing He is in control and our citizenship in His kingdom is sealed and sure.

Nov 11

Chuckle: *"Why did your mom marry your dad?"*
An elementary school child replied, "My grandma says that Mom didn't have her thinking cap on."
Quote: *"When I believe, I am no longer a mere man, I am already a son of God."* ~ Carlo Carretto

God's Unconditional Acceptance

"God sent Christ to make peace between himself and us, and he has given us the work of making peace (reconciliation) between himself and others" (2 Corinthians 5:18 CEV).

Every one of us has a strong desire to be loved and accepted—to be found worthy of inclusion. Just to know we are included in a group, organization, or team contributes to our sense of self-worth and perceived value to others. When we think about our sinful condition, it's hard to imagine that Almighty God, the Creator of the Universe, has accepted us as we are and desires a personal love relationship with us. He wants this relationship regardless of our past sins—He accepts us as precious to Him even with all our "warts" and other imperfections.

God not only has accepted us, He took the initiative to let us know how much He loves us through His Son, Jesus Christ. Through Christ, He brings us to Himself and nothing can ever break that bond of love or take away that sense of peace that defies human understanding. Through faith in Christ and the sealing of His Holy Spirit, we have the assurance of an eternal and unchanging relationship with God.

Because we have been accepted by—and made right with—God, we have the responsibility to grant unconditional acceptance to others regardless of their race, ethnicity, or social standing. When God accepted you and me, it was unconditional. There is nothing we can do to make God love us more, or nothing we can do to make God love us less. If we could only accept others with this same kind of love, we would not be so hesitant to tell others the good news of Jesus Christ.

Evangelist Vance Havner, preaching at the Moody Bible Institute's Founder's Week in 1974, stated: *"Evangelism is to Christianity what veins are to our bodies. You can cut Christianity anywhere and it'll bleed evangelism. Evangelism is vascular, it's our business. Talk about majoring in evangelism, you might as well talk about a doctor majoring on healing. That's our business."*

If our business is to be evangelism, we must see all people through the eyes of Jesus, and unconditionally accept them as Jesus does. When God reconciled us to Himself, He gave us the privilege of reconciling people to Him. *"And He has committed to us the message of reconciliation. We are therefore Christ's ambassadors, as though God were making his appeal through us"* (2 Corinthians 5:19-20 NIV).

Oh, that we would be as accepting of others as God has been of us, and turn that acceptance into bold sharing the love of Christ.

Nov 12

Chuckle: *"Inflation is growing," a young man said to a friend. "Yesterday, in a restaurant, I ordered a twenty-five dollar steak and told them to put it on my credit card—and it fit."*

Quote: *"Make us to choose the harder right instead of the easier wrong, and never be content with a half-truth when the whole truth can be won."* ~ Col. C. E. Wheat

Wishful Thinking and Integrity

"People with integrity have firm footing, but those who follow crooked paths will slip and fall" (Proverbs 10:9 NLT). *"The integrity of the upright guides them, but the unfaithful are destroyed by their duplicity"* (Proverbs 11:3 NIV).

Words defining integrity often include honesty, truthfulness, uprightness, honorable, probity, etc. These essential traits are certainly present in a person of integrity.

However, I believe integrity, in its broadest definition, also includes other critical traits. Our passage says the integrity of the upright guides them. This makes sense when we look at other meanings of integrity. It also means completeness or wholeness, a complete person not lacking in any component of integrity, an undivided or unbroken state, tried and proven.

Todays' quote is from the West Point Cadet's Prayer. As you read it carefully, I'm sure you will notice that the prayer asks God for strength to display other essential character traits not normally included in a common definition of integrity. These include discernment of right and wrong, the ability to make wise decisions, courage in the face of physical danger, intolerance of mediocrity, and a hunger for the whole truth.

Now that we have identified the character traits in a person of complete integrity, listen to the following by General Omar N. Bradley, who, in 1949, became the first Chairman of the Joint Chiefs of Staff.

The Cadet's Prayer contains a warning of two of the worst pitfalls into which men—beset by events—can fall: the loose, wishful thinking that causes some people to hide themselves from the facts (reality); and the willingness to compromise principles for expedient gain.

Wishful thinking is the easy and smoothly paved road to compromise. Knowing that the right road is also the harder one, we have an all-too-human tendency to choose the easier way. And, of course, the justification for our choice becomes a simple task. For we have great powers of rationalization when it comes to proving to ourselves that we have made either a "reasonable" or "practical" choice.

It is futile for us, as Christians, to waste time in wishful thinking—wishing that things were different in our society and the world. Instead, we should fall on our knees before God confessing and repenting of our sins and calling on Him to *"make us choose the harder right instead of the easier wrong, and never be content with a half-truth when the whole truth can be won."*

Each of us should strive to be a person of complete integrity as the Holy Spirit empowers us, and allow that integrity to guide us to make right harder choices, not just the easier reasonable or practical choices.

Nov 13

Chuckle: *"For a saint to desire to sin is as ridiculous as a rodeo where cowboys ride calves to rope horses. Not only is the experience unnatural, it is extremely unproductive!"*

Quote: *"Sin is like a man's beard. Although we daily destroy its manifestations, it constantly reappears."* ~ Unknown Source

Winning the Sin Battle

"Direct my footsteps according to your word; let no sin rule over me" (Psalm 119:133 NIV).

As we think about winning the sin battle, I'm reminded of another passage from the Psalms about the importance of God's Word in this battle. *"Your word is a lamp to my feet and a light for my path. I have taken an oath and confirmed it, that I will follow your righteous laws"* (Psalm 119:105-106 NIV).

In our basic passage, the psalmist asked God to guide his footsteps so that his life would not be controlled (ruled) by sin. In the second passage, he acknowledged dependence upon God's Word to light his way so that he could avoid Satan's temptation to sin. In both instances, he knew the importance of keeping God's precepts uppermost in his mind.

Sin is not a popular subject with many people today. However, if you are a Christian you know that we live in a constant struggle with our old sinful nature. Notice that the psalmist did not promise God he would never sin. Rather, he asked for God's help to keep him from being ruled by sin. He knew he could not defeat sin without God's help. .

Near Watsonville, California, there is a creek that has a strange name: Salsipuedes Creek. Salsi puedes is Spanish for "Get out of it, if you can." The creek is lined with quicksand, and the

story is that many years ago, in the early days of California, a Mexican laborer fell into the quicksand. A Spaniard, riding by on a horse, saw him and yelled out to him, "Salsi puedes!" which was not very helpful to the struggling worker. The creek has been so named ever since. That is what the flesh (our own strength) is like. We struggle to get out of the effects of our own sinful nature—but we cannot on our own. ~ Illustrations for Biblical Preaching, Edited by Michael P. Green

In our own strength, we can never win the battle against sin. As a Christian, however, *"You are not controlled by the sinful nature but by the Spirit, if the Spirit of God lives in you"* (Romans 8:9a NIV). We must spend time in God's Word and in prayer, and allow the indwelling Holy Spirit to provide us the strength to avoid the habit of sinning. Sinning should become abhorrent to us. It should be against our new nature in Christ. *"No one who lives in him (Christ) keeps on (continues) sinning"* (1 John 3:6 NIV). Willfully sinning is unnatural for the Christian and should never become a way of life—a lifestyle.

When we do sin, we will be miserable and should immediately turn to God and ask His forgiveness (See 1 John 1:9). If we are walking closely with Jesus, we will not desire to deliberately sin. But sin can creep into our lives and control us if we are not being controlled by the Spirit of God.

Nov 14

Chuckle: *A lawyer and a doctor were at the gym. The doctor complained that while he exercises, people always ask for advice. "What should I do?"*

"Well," said the lawyer, "when you give advice, send a bill." In a few days, the doctor got a bill from the lawyer.

Quote: *"He is truly great that is little in himself and that maketh no account of any height of honors."* ~ Thomas à Kempis

Vanity and Conceit

"Do not think of yourself more highly than you ought, but think of yourself with sober judgment, in accordance with the measure of faith God has given you" (Romans 12:3 NIV).

Vanity is defined as "the quality of being vain or conceited about oneself; excessive pride in one's appearance, qualities, abilities, achievements, etc." It's ironic that vanity also means a condition of no real value—worthless.

Many of the world's problems can be traced to powerful people filled with vanity and conceit. These include brutal dictators and other cruel despots. I'm reminded of a saying that goes something like this: "Power corrupts, and absolute power corrupts absolutely." Such people sometimes see themselves as above the law or rules that apply to everyone else. They see themselves as a cut above those over whom they have influence.

"But lasting good has always been wrought by those who answer to Thomas à Kempis's description (our quote), and see themselves infinitely small—as a man feels when he stands alone in darkness, looking up to the starry skies." ~ Eric Johnston

Those who are infatuated with their perceived importance

and power often prey on the powerless. Such an attitude should never be found in a Christian regardless of his or her position of leadership. Our passage warns Christians not to think too highly of themselves, but to evaluate ourselves based on the degree of faith God has given us.

The minds of wise Christians have been transformed by the power of the Holy Spirit who re-educates, renews, and redirects their hearts and minds. Great people are loving, humble, compassionate, and quietly wise—no matter what great deeds they perform or the high honors they receive. Jesus said to His disciples, *". . . whoever wants to be great among you must be your servant"* (Matthew 20:26 NIV).

An old fable of Aesop tells of the fox and the crow. A crow once stole a piece of meat. The fox, who wanted the meat, began to compliment the crow. First he complimented the beauty of her black feathers. Then he complimented the beauty of her form. Finally he complimented her singing voice and asked to hear her sing. The crow was so overcome by the praise that she opened her mouth to sing and dropped the meat, which the fox promptly picked up and ate. Our experience tells us that such vanity is not reserved for crows.

Nov 15

Chuckle: *"I eat out occasionally, but I never go to the same restaurant twice," a man remarked.*

To which his friend replied, "I don't leave a tip either!"

Quote: *"When you cannot trust God, you cannot trust anything; and when you cannot trust anything you get the condition of the world as it is today."* ~ Basil King

In What or Whom Do You Trust?

"Some trust in chariots and some in horses, but we trust in the name of the LORD our God" (Psalm 20:7 NIV). *"The LORD Almighty is with us; the God of Jacob is our fortress"* (Psalm 46:11 NIV).

The United States is perhaps the greatest military power the world has ever known. The destructive force available to us as a nation is almost beyond comprehension. However, history is replete with accounts of powerful nations who were brought to their knees not by superior military power but by moral corruption and decay from within. As a "super power," it's tempting to see ourselves as invincible and place our trust in the power we have created rather than in the One who is the Super Power.

In the Old Testament, there are many accounts of Israel flourishing as a nation and then, because of their sin and disobedience to God, declining into a weak nation of helpless people dominated and enslaved by more powerful and evil nations. What makes us Americans think we are any different? What makes us think nothing or anyone can bring us down? If my sense of the mood in this country is correct, we may not be nearly as cocky and certain of our invincibility as we once were. Could God be placing these doubts in our minds to make us renew our individual and national dependence upon Him instead of our military and economic power? In what or whom do you trust?

Down through history, nations have risen to great power and boasted about their armies and weapons only to see that power crumble and vanish in the dust. In our passage, David was concerned about this very thing. He knew that the true greatness of a nation was measured not by the power of its weaponry, but by the quality of its worship—trusting in God's power rather than military power.

If you share King David's concern as it relates to our beloved country, perhaps you and each of us should be asking, "what can I do to help ensure the greatness of our nation is preserved?" I know you are familiar with 2 Chronicles 7:14, but it bears repeating here. *"If my people (that's you and me), who are called by my name, will humble themselves and pray and seek my face and turn from their wicked ways, then will I hear from heaven and will forgive their sin and heal their land."*

Wouldn't it be wonderful if every Christian in America would model his/her life after this passage? If we did so and once more placed our trust in God rather than ourselves, we would be opening the door for Him to do miraculous things. Maybe our humble and repentant hearts would convince God that it would be worth His while to heal and restore America to its former God-given greatness.

Nov 16

Chuckle: *A little boy asked, "Why don't you come to my church next Sunday?"*

"Because I belong to another abomination," the answer came.

Quote: *"The blessed and inviting truth is that God is the most winsome of all beings and in our worship of Him we should find unspeakable pleasure."* ~ A. W. Tozer

Preparing for Worship

Jesus said, *"God is spirit, and his worshipers must worship in spirit and in truth"* (John 4:24 NIV). *"Come, let us bow down in worship, let us kneel before the Lord our Maker"* (Psalm 95:6 NIV).

As you look forward during the week to participating in worship services on Sunday, how do you prepare your heart and mind for worshiping with your brothers and sisters in Christ? For our Sunday worship to be what God desires, spiritual preparation during the week is a must. Daily private worship through prayer, Bible study, confession, praise and thanksgiving will prepare your spirit for congregational worship on the Lord's day.

Worship is not a performance to bring attention to those on stage, be they preachers, singers, instrumentalists, or laypersons. Worship is an offering to God and must be done privately from the heart. It is not visible to the human eyes—it is done in the spirit. For our worship to be pleasing and acceptable to God, it must be genuine and emanate from the heart.

God is spirit, not a physical being whom we can see and

touch. He exists in a different realm or plane from humans and He is not subject to the same limitations of a physical body like ours. Our relationship with God is deeply personal and He can be worshiped only at the intensely personal level. We worship God's Spirit from deep within our human spirits as we are led by the Holy Spirit. Worship in Spirit and truth requires spiritual preparation.

How can we prepare our hearts for congregational worship? As we go through the week, we can spend time daily alone in prayer and meditation on God's Word. We can confess and ask God to forgive specific sins in our lives (See 1 John 1:9). We can look forward with excitement to joining God's people in worship on Sunday. We can pray for the pastor, the music worship leader, and all the other worshipers. We can serve the needs of others. We can ask the Holy Spirit to help us restore any broken relationships that detract from our ability to worship. We can recognize the benefits of public worship and anticipate that God will transform our lives each time we come together.

As we prepare our hearts throughout the week, we will discover that our worship becomes never ending. We will come to better understand what Paul meant when he said we should pray without ceasing. We will come to realize that we are worshiping our Lord continuously seven days a week, not just on Sunday morning. Then we will be prepared to join our brothers and sisters in meaningful, uplifting, and life-changing worship on Sunday.

God will work miracles in the hearts of those who have adequately prepared for worship.

Nov 17

Chuckle: *"Birthdays are good for you—the more you have, the longer you live."*

Quote: *"Hope means expectancy when things are otherwise hopeless."* ~ G.K. Chesterton

Helping Others Deal with Tragedy

"Praise be to the God and Father of our Lord Jesus Christ, the Father of compassion and the God of comfort, who comforts us in all our troubles so that we can comfort those in any trouble with the comfort we ourselves have received from God" (2 Corinthians 1:3-4 NIV).

When someone close to us experiences a tragic loss, such as the death of a loved one, we feel inadequate to express our feelings as we grope for the right words. We hope to make the tragedy a little more bearable by our presence and support.

Because of our human inadequacies, there's only one place to go for consolation and comfort—God's Word. How can we minister to those experiencing tragedies in their lives?
We can intercede for them in prayer. I love this prayer.

"O Lord, who is the comforter of your children, the God of love and tenderness, I pray for those who mourn at this time. We need not tell their sorrow to you. In the stillness of our hearts we ask for them your sustaining grace. Be their stay in this sore trial; the strength of the fainting heart and the Light of the darkened home. Open their eyes to see the Father's House on high, and may they feel assured that the departed has found a better life, and a more perfect rest in you. Almighty God, may this visitation of death be your voice speaking to us, and may it minister to a truer and holier life in our souls. May our passing

days be rich in those things which death cannot take from us; and may you strengthen us to live that life of faith and righteousness, of love and peace, which makes the last earthly change but a step nearer to you, our Everlasting Refuge and Home. Hear us for your mercy's sake, through Jesus Christ our Lord." ~ John Hunter

We can help meet their spiritual needs by encouraging them to turn to God for comfort, strength, and peace rather than being angry with God. *"The Lord is my strength, my shield from every danger. I trust him with all my heart. He helps me, and my heart is filled with joy. I burst out in songs of thanksgiving"* (Psalm 28:7 NLT).

We can help meet their physical needs in practical ways. *"When God's children are in need, be the one to help them out. And get into the habit of inviting guests home for dinner or, if they need lodging, for the night"* (Romans 12:13 NLT). You can help greatly by your compassion, warm hospitality, and other practical ministries.

We can help meet their emotional needs by making ourselves available and by spending time with them. We can be a shoulder to lean on and cry on. We can offer a sympathetic ear to their expressions of pain. *"When others are happy, be happy with them. if they are sad, share their sorrow"* (Romans 12:15 NLT). *"Share each other's troubles and problems, and in this way obey the law of Christ"* (Galatians 6:2 NLT).

Hurting people need empathy and understanding rather than advice.

Nov 18

Chuckle: *"If the best things in life are free, why are the next best things so expensive?"*

Quote: *Virtue isn't virtue unless it slams up against vice so, consequently, your virtue is not real virtue until it's been tested ... and tempted."* ~ Unknown Source

Testing and Disciplining

"But He knows the way that I take; when he has tested me, I will come forth as gold" (Job 23:10 NIV).

According to the Scriptures, God tests us and disciplines us as His children. Sometimes it's difficult to discern the difference. Generally speaking, God's punishment comes as a result of sin, while testing comes to determine the dimensions of our faith. When God allows difficult and challenging situations to enter your life, the first question you should ask yourself is: "Do I have unconfessed and unforgiven sin in my life?" If the answer is "yes," then you should consider the possibility that God is disciplining you for your sins—to draw you back to Himself through your confession and repentance.

Otherwise, it may be that God is testing you to strengthen and prepare you for a special service He desires you to perform. In either case, an appropriate question is: "Lord, what are you trying to teach me in this situation?"

Testing. God tested Abraham's faith and obedience (See Genesis 22:1 NIV) by commanding him to sacrifice his son, Isaac. This was to determine if Abraham would obey God unconditionally regardless of what God asked of him. You may recall that after Abraham had proven his willingness to obey God by sacrificing his own son, God said to him: *"Do not lay a* *hand on the boy . . . do not do anything to him. Now I know that you fear God, because you have not withheld from me your son, your only son"* (Genesis 22:12 NIV).

Because of his faith, God promised to bless Abraham and the whole world through his descendants. Through this testing, God was preparing Abraham for greater tasks for His kingdom. Testing burns off the dross of faithlessness, indifference, and disobedience in our lives in the same way that fire purifies gold. It is designed to make us instruments that God can use for His purposes.

Discipline: God punishes us for the same reasons you punish your children—because you love them and want the best for them. *"My child, don't ignore it when the Lord disciplines you, and don't be discouraged when he corrects you. For the Lord disciplines those he loves, and he punishes those he accepts as his children"* (Hebrews 12:5b-6 NLT). Who do you think loves his child more—the parent who allows the child to do what will harm him, or the one who corrects, trains, and even punishes the child to help him learn what is right? *"Don't make your children angry by the way you treat them. Rather, bring them up with the discipline and instruction approved by the Lord"* (Ephesians 6:4 NLT).

God's discipline may not be pleasant, but it's a wonderful sign of His deep and unconditional love for us. *"No discipline seems pleasant at the time, but painful. Later on, however, it produces a harvest of righteousness and peace for those who have been trained by it"* (Hebrews 12:11 NIV).

Nov 19

Chuckle: More fun with the English language: *"After a number of Novocain injections, my jaw got number."*

Quote: *"The whole Christian life is that we are totally one with each other in the church, that Christ has given himself totally to us in oneness."* ~ Fr Peter Ball

Unity Among Christians

"Always keep yourselves united in the Holy Spirit , and bind yourselves together with peace. We are all one body, we have the same Spirit, and we have all been called to the same glorious future" (Ephesians 4:3-4 NLT).

Dr. Martin Luther King, Jr., had a dream that our nation would truly come together around the concept that all people are created equal, and that this national unity would usher in a spirit of good will and understanding within our citizenry—regardless of race, ethnicity, or social standing. This is a worthy goal for each of us and for our nation.

We know that Dr. King's dream will only come to fruition when we allow God to change each of our hearts. Such unity and understanding can never be legislated, mandated, or dictated, but must grow from within our hearts. Unfortunately, we often see a lack of unity even among Christians, and until this situation is rectified, the full attainment of Dr. King's dream for our nation will remain distant and unrealized.

In our passage, Paul is pleading for unity within the body of Christ—the church. When believers live in unity, it is a beautiful thing to behold and an amazing testimony to the power of God's love and His Holy Spirit. Perhaps each of us should do some self-evaluation of our attitudes toward

Christian unity.

One of the Holy Spirit's most important roles is to build unity as He leads us and teaches us. But we must be willing to have our hearts and attitudes changed—toward both fellow believers and other people in general.

This can only happen when we keep our focus on God rather than ourselves and our own likes and dislikes. Dissention within the church often occurs over the most petty and insignificant issues. When a disagreement is not dealt with, it will grow, fester, and become a major source of conflict. When a brother or sister does something differently than the way you would do it, immediately stop, think, and pray about the disunity that will occur if you are unforgiving and make it a big issue.

We must all remember that we who belong to Christ are a part of one body (church) under one Head, Jesus Christ. None of us enjoys a higher standing with God than everyone else. We are all equal in God's sight and problems arise when our sight and God's sight are not the same.

Jesus prayed to the Father that *"they (we) may be one as we (He and the Father) are one: . . . May they be brought to complete unity to let the world know that you sent me . ."* (John 17:22b-23 NIV). As we unify in love around a common purpose, we can be a positive influence for unity in our world.

Nov 20

Chuckle: *A wife to her husband: "That suit looks nice on you dear. I just hope you don't decide to inhale!"*

Quote: *"God creates out of the absolute superabundance of his mercy and love."* ~ George Florovsky

You Are Wonderfully Made

"You are worthy, our Lord and God, to receive glory . . . for you created all things, and by your will they were created and have their being" (Revelation 4:11 NIV).

Are there times when you feel people, even those closest to you, just don't understand you? They don't have a clue about who you are and what talents and abilities you possess? To fully understand a person, one would have to become that person and live as they live. When we think about how difficult it is to really know someone and fully appreciate their unique abilities and personality, it should remind us once again of the amazing attributes of God. He knows you intimately because He created you physically, emotionally, and spiritually.

You are you—a unique creation of God. *"For you created my inmost being; you knit me together in my mother's womb. I praise you because I am fearfully and wonderfully made"* (Psalms 139:13-14 NIV). There is no other exactly like you. As your Creator, He made you to suit Himself and knows everything about you.

You are God's treasured possession. *"You are a chosen people, . . . a people belonging to God, that you may declare the praises of him who called you out of darkness into his wonderful light"* (1 Peter 2:9 NIV). You are uniquely valuable and beautiful in His eyes. When God created you, He made no mistakes. You are just as He wanted you to be, and everything about you is lovely and precious to Him

You are a member of God's own family/household. *"Consequently, you are . . . fellow citizens with God's people and members of God's household"* (Ephesians 2:19 NIV). Because of God's amazing love, grace, and mercy you have become a precious member of God's family—if you have trusted Christ as Savior and Lord.

You are gifted by God with great potential for service. *"We have different gifts, according to the grace given us"* (Romans 12:6 NIV). These gifts and abilities are to be used as instruments of service to bless the lives of others for the glory of God.

The next time you look at yourself in a mirror, please remember that God made you, loves you, and wants you to know how perfectly you were created. Therefore, all of us should praise and honor God because He is the Creator and Sustainer of all things.

"In order to create there must be a dynamic force, and what force is more potent than love." ~ Igor Stravinsky

Nov 21

Chuckle: *Doctor to the patient: "Your recovery was a miracle!"*

Patient: "Praise God! Now I don't have to pay you."

Quote: *"To believe only possibilities is not faith, but mere philosophy."* ~ Sir Thomas Brown

Living by Faith

"What is faith? It is the confident assurance that what we hope for is going to happen. It is the evidence of things we cannot see. God gave his approval to people in days of old because of their faith... So, you see it is impossible to please God without faith..." (Hebrews 11:1-2, 6 NLT).

The word "faith" can have several different shades of meaning depending upon its usage. But let's focus on the definition found in our Hebrews passage. The Holy Spirit inspired writer of Hebrews focuses on the kind of faith exhibited by righteous people down through the ages, some of whom are identified later in Hebrews 11.

First, faith is being absolutely certain about the person (reality) of God and who He is. By faith, we know God is real even though He is unseen by our human eyes. We know He is real by observing His creation, by the ways He revealed Himself to the prophets of old, by His revelation through His Son, Jesus Christ, and finally, through the totality of His written Word as illuminated by the Holy Spirit. But the greatest indication of who God is comes from our own individual experience with Him working in our lives.

Faith begins by believing that God is who He says He is—that He is real and that He loves us and desires to interact with us. Faith is also the unwavering conviction that the unseen—but anticipated—mighty acts of God will bring more indescribable surprises than our finite imaginations can ever see. *"No eye has seen, no ear has heard, and no mind has imagined what God has prepared for those who love him"* (1 Corinthians 2:9 NLT).

Second, faith is being confident that God will fulfill all His promises. Faith, at this level, believes God will make good on His promises even though we may not see their complete fulfilment in our lifetimes. This is how we demonstrate the kind of faith God desires of us. Abel, Enoch, Noah, Abraham, Sarah, and *"All these faithful ones died without receiving what God had promised them, but they saw it all from a distance and welcomed the promises of God"* (Hebrews 11:13 NLT). Even though they died without receiving all that God had promised them, they never wavered in their anticipation of a better place—their heavenly home and future rewards.

The kind of faith by which God wants us to live inevitably results in total commitment and faithful obedience to our Lord. *"Foolish man! When will you ever learn that faith that does not result in good deeds is useless . . . So you see, we are made right with God by what we do, not by faith alone"* (James 2:20,24 NLT).

In summary, living by faith is believing that God is real—that He will keep His promises—and obeying His commands to serve Him by serving others. Faith is proven by our actions.

Nov 22

Chuckle: (church bulletin blooper) *"The pastor will preach his farewell message, after which the choir will sing, 'Break Forth Into Joy.'"*

Quote: *"You can judge a man pretty well by whether—if given a choice—he would ask for a lighter burden or a stronger back."* ~ Unknown Source

Choices Matter

". . . choose for yourselves this day whom you will serve . . . . But as for me and my household, we will (choose to) serve the Lord" (Joshua 24:15 NIV).

Each day we are faced with a series of choices that determine the course of our lives and often the lives of others. Joshua made his choice to serve the Lord. This is a basic choice each of us must make. However, every day we make hundreds of lesser choices that not only impact our lives but the lives of those around us. An eternal perspective on life's choices is to know how to choose wisely.

Are your choices based on selfish motives? *"Do nothing from selfishness or empty conceit, but in humility consider others better than yourselves. Each of you should look not only to your own interests, but also to the interests of others"* (Philippians 2:3-4 NIV). Who do you think about when it comes to making choices/decisions? Is it "what's in it for me?" "Will this benefit me?" "How will this affect me?" Are you always looking out for old number one? The above passage tells us that the interests of others should be more important to us than our own when we make choices.

Are your choices based on material things? *"Let your*

character be free from the love of money. . ." (Hebrews 13:5 NIV). *"For the love of money is a root of all kinds of evil. Some people, eager for money, have wandered away from the faith, and pierced themselves with many griefs"* (1 Timothy 6:10 NIV). This passage is often misinterpreted. It is not money or possessions that are the problem—it is our infatuation with them. It is our all-consuming preoccupation with acquiring money and possessions that grieves our Lord. They can become the most important and treasured things in life to us. God's Word encourages hard work and good management. Having possessions, or not, is not the issue. It's our attitude toward them, and how we use them.

Are your choices based on spiritual compromise? *"Religion that God our Father accepts as pure and faultless is this: to look after orphans and widows in their distress and to keep oneself from being polluted (or stained) by the world"* (James 1:27 NIV). As we make choices in life, they should be from a different motivation. You've probably seen the letters WWJD (**W**hat **W**ould **J**esus **D**o). These letters remind us to make decisions from an eternal spiritual perspective, no matter how great or small these decisions might be.

To make choices that are pleasing to our Lord and benefit others should be our goal.

Nov 23

Chuckle: *A preacher was writing a sermon and his son asked, "Daddy, does the Lord tell you what to say?"*

"Of course He does!"

"Then why do you keep scratching some of it out?"

Quote: *"By making choices consistent with eternal truth you will develop righteous character."* ~ Richard G. Scott

Choices Reveal Character

"Whoever can be trusted with very little can also be trusted with much, and whoever is dishonest with very little will also be dishonest with much" (Luke 16:10 NIV).

Every day God allows each Christian to be tested with a series of small choices. "Little things mean a lot." You might say, "I would never rob a bank or swindle someone out of their possessions. However, I might choose to cheat a little on my income tax—or be less than completely honest in a business deal. After all, doesn't everyone operate that way?"

Some seem to think it's OK to be less than honest in relatively insignificant matters—as long as we are honest in the major transactions of life. What does this attitude say about our character? What are we teaching our children and grandchildren about character? What does God think of us when we compromise our integrity? Jesus teaches us the importance of making good choices even in what we perceive as the most minor of situations.

In our passage, Jesus teaches us that our character will determine our assignments from God. In a parable, Jesus said: *"Well done, my good servant! . . . because you have been trustworthy in a very small matter, take charge of ten cities"*

(Luke 19:17 NIV). If you feel your place of service in your church is not as important to God as someone else's, perhaps you will want to think again. There is no insignificant ministry to others in Jesus' name. Jesus made His point like this: *"I tell you the truth, anyone who gives you a cup of water in my name because you belong to Christ will certainly not lose his reward"* (Mark 9:41 NIV).

Right choices and faithfulness in the small tasks develop Christian character and prepare you for even greater responsibilities. God is more interested in your availability and faithfulness than He is with your opinion of the relative importance of what He has asked you to do. He wants us to maintain our integrity at all times and make godly decisions in all matters, whether great or small.

My prayer is that each of us will take another look at how we make daily choices and decisions in light of these passages of Scripture. The daily choices we make reveal our true character. Someone has said, *"Your ideal is what you wish you were. Your reputation is what people say you are. Your character is what you are."*

Nov 24

Chuckle: *A minister asked a group of children why they loved God. After several answers, one little boy said, "Sir. I guess it just runs in our family."*

Quote: *"God's love for us is constant and will not diminish, but he cannot rescue us from the painful results caused by wrong choices."* ~ Marvin J. Ashton

Choices Have Consequences

"Do not be deceived: God cannot be mocked. A man reaps what he sows. The one who sows to please his sinful nature, from that nature will reap destruction; the one who sows to please the Spirit, from the Spirit will reap eternal life" (Galatians 6:7 NIV).

I remember an old 1950's television show called "Truth or Consequences." Contestants were asked silly trick questions which they almost never answered correctly. The host then told them that since they had failed to tell the truth, they would have to pay the consequences. The consequences were often embarrassing and humiliating—all in good fun of course.

Unfortunately, there is nothing humorous about making bad choices in life which can have serious consequences. It is a natural law to reap what one sows, and it is true in all areas of life. In the same way that a crop is harvested from a seed placed in the ground, every choice you make in life will reap its consequences. If you do not know Christ as Savior, each time you make a choice not to accept Him, you risk eternal consequences. *". . . . how shall we escape if we ignore such a great salvation?"* (Hebrews 2:3 NIV).

If you are a born again Christian, you will want to make choices that please God and bless others. However, sometimes we will make wrong choices resulting in sin. When this happens we must quickly confess our sins to God with an attitude of genuine repentance and receive forgiveness and cleansing (See1 John 1:9). But God's forgiveness does not always mean the consequences of our actions are removed.

I'm reminded of King David who committed the sins of adultery and murder. God forgave him and used him mightily, but the consequences of David's choices (sins) brought much pain and disappointment to him and his family throughout his life. As a genuine born again Christian, you will never lose your salvation, but your bad choices can certainly bring pain to you and others close to you. Also, wrong choices in service to your Lord can result in your missing out on the joy and other rewards God wants to give you. *"If any man's work is burned up, he shall suffer loss; but he himself shall be saved, yet so as through fire"* (1 Corinthians 3:15 NIV).

Right choices will bring God's blessings and rewards. When we trust Christ as Lord and Savior, we have God's promise of eternal life and the best possible life here on earth. If we make the right choices as Christians, God will reward us. If not, we forfeit those rewards. *"For we must all appear before the judgment seat of Christ, that each one may receive what is due him for the things done while in the body, whether good or bad"* (2 Corinthians 5:10 NIV).

Nov 25

Chuckle: *While driving down the freeway, a senior citizen answered his phone. He heard his wife's voice urgently warning him, "Herman, I just heard on the news that there's a car going the wrong way on Interstate 77. Please be careful!"*

"Heck," said Herman, "It's not just one car. It's hundreds of them!"

Quote: *"When a man is content with the testimony of his own conscience, he does not care to shine with the light of another's praise."* ~ St Bernard of Clairvaux

Living with a Clear Conscience

"Let us draw near to God with a sincere heart in full assurance of faith, having our hearts sprinkled to cleanse us from a guilty conscience . . ." (Hebrews 10:22 NIV). *"They must keep hold of the deep truths of the faith with a pure (clear) conscience"* (1 Timothy 3:9 NIV).

As a boy, I loved to play basketball. At one point we lived a short distance from my school which had a gymnasium. Even though the gym was off limits during non-school hours, I had learned how to get into the gym in such a way that no one would know I had been there. One day, my dad confronted me and asked if I had been in the gym. I knew I had done wrong and hoped that, after I confessed, I would receive dad's forgiveness—which came after a fierce tongue-lashing.

After receiving my dad's forgiveness, my guilty conscience faded away because I knew he loved me even though I had done wrong. Genuine forgiveness is the only cure for a guilty conscience.

As a follower of Christ, we were given a clear conscience

when all our sins were forgiven and we were made pure and acceptable before God. He cleansed us and made pure in His sight. I pray you have experienced such cleansing because you have trusted Jesus Christ as your Savior and Lord. Even though we are given a clear conscience, it's up to us to keep it that way every day of our lives.

In 1 John 1:9, God lets us in on a fantastic provision He has made for His children. He knows we commit sins every day we live, even though we should strive not to do so. In our weakness, He promises: *"If we confess our sins, he is faithful and just and will forgive us our sins and purify us from all unrighteousness."* As we spend time each day with our Lord reading His Word and in prayer, He sensitizes our consciences to recognize even the most obscure sins that keep us from being what God wants us to be. As we become aware of each sin in our lives, and the pangs of a guilty conscience set in, we should confess our sins and ask forgiveness. Then we should pray for the strength and grace to help us not repeat them.

In the same way that our consciences are sensitized when we spend time with our Lord, the opposite is true. Our consciences can become insensitive and dulled, and we are free of guilt and remorse. If there are sins in your life with which you have become comfortable and no longer feel guilty about, please draw near to God, confess those sins and seek forgiveness. This is how spiritual renewal starts and where you can begin to live each day with a clear conscience.

Nov 26

Chuckle: *Father: "You have four Ds and a C on your report card!"*

Son: "I know. I think I concentrated too much on one subject."

Quote: *"Most of us follow our conscience as we follow a wheelbarrow. We push it in front of us in the direction we want to go."* ~ Billy Graham

A Defiled Conscience

"Everything is pure to those whose hearts are pure. But nothing is pure to those who are corrupt and unbelieving, because their minds and consciences are defiled" (Titus 1:15 NLT).

The human conscience intrigues me. The word "conscience" describes an inner sense of right and wrong—a feeling that guides us away from doing bad things and persuades us to do the right things. For example, "His conscience bothered him after he told a lie." The question I want us to consider here is, how do our consciences become sufficiently trained to be reliable as a guide for righteous living?

The definition of "conscience' that I gave in the first paragraph does not take into account the proposition that some consciences are corrupted and are not reliable as a guide for discerning right and wrong. This is evident when evil people do terrible things without guilt or remorse. Their lack of conscience causes them to do evil things without regretting their actions. *"He that loses his conscience has nothing else worth keeping."* ~ Isaac Walton

When addressing false teachers in the last days, Paul writes, *"They will follow lying spirits and teachings that come from demons. These teachers are hypocrites and liars. They pretend to be religious, but their consciences are dead (seared)"* (1 Timothy 4:1-2 NLT). In our first passage, Paul deals with the consciences of the corrupt and unbelieving. But Christians are also subject to having their consciences hijacked and corrupted by the evil one so that they become his instruments of destruction in our lives and Christ's church.

I have witnessed professing "Christians" who were guilty of hateful and destructive actions toward other believers, and they showed no regret or remorse. It was as if they thought their actions were acceptable to God, and even directed by God. But we know God is never the author of such actions or discord. Obviously, it is God's Word and the indwelling Holy Spirit that trains and sensitizes our consciences to guide us into righteous living. But when we drift away and stop praying and meditating on God's Word, Satan will begin to convince us that the world's way is better than God's way; and the voice of our consciences will become weaker and weaker and our sensitivity to right and wrong will gradually diminish.

I believe every born again believer has at least a rudimentary spiritual conscience. That still small voice within us is our spiritual conscience. As we grow spiritually, God continues to sensitize our consciences—a work in progress over a lifetime if we allow Him access to the innermost depths of our hearts and minds.

Nov 27

Chuckle: *"The latest survey shows that three out of four people make up 75% of the population."*

Quote: *"The man who loses his conscience has nothing left that is worth keeping."* ~ Isaac Walton

Reliable Conscience

"They demonstrate that God's law is written within them, for their own consciences either accuse them or tell them they are doing what is right" (Romans 2:15 NLT). *"Everything is pure to those whose hearts are pure. But nothing is pure to those who are corrupt and unbelieving, because their minds and consciences are defiled"* (Titus 1:15 NLT). *"They pretend to be religious, but their consciences are dead"* (1 Timothy 4:2 NLT).

Perhaps you have noticed that we don't have to teach a child to lie, cheat, and steal. It seems they already know how to do these things when they are born. No, we have to teach them what is right as they grow—to be kind, caring, honest, and unselfish. As they are taught, their consciences become reliable moral compasses in their lives. If they are not trained to distinguish between right and wrong and to respect right over wrong, their undeveloped consciences will be of no value to them in life.

Our consciences can be trained. If we use God's Word as the basis for bringing up our children, they will know right and wrong from God's viewpoint. But if they are raised by parents whose own consciences were never trained by God's values, what can we expect from the children. Every day we hear of murders, robberies, rapes, assaults, corrupt business deals, and other crimes committed by people who show no remorse except for having been caught. Evidently, their consciences serve no useful purpose.

In our Romans passage, we see that "God's law was written within them," and because this was true, their consciences were reliable to accuse them of wrong and to affirm their doing right. Each of us should pray to God for such a conscience. However, once we have a conscience that pleases God, we must listen to and heed our consciences or they will become increasingly less reliable.

"The conscience is like a sharp square peg in our hearts. If we are confronted by a questionable situation, that square begins to turn, and its corners cut into our hearts, warning us with an inward sensation against doing whatever confronts us. If the conscience is ignored time after time, the corners of the square are gradually worn down, and it virtually becomes a circle. When that circle turns within our hearts, there is no inner sensation of warning, and we are left without a conscience."
~ Unknown Source

Our consciences need to remain sensitive to God's standards of morality. In our 1 Timothy passage, we see false teachers whose consciences are dead and useless. Have you noticed that if you override your conscience and do something wrong, it becomes easier to do that wrong again and again?

Your conscience gradually becomes seared and less of a factor in determining your behavior.

Nov 28

Chuckle: *"If you think nobody cares if you're alive, try missing a couple of car payments!!"*

Quote: *"Do not be anxious about anything, but in everything, by prayer and petition, with thanksgiving, present your requests to God. And the peace of God, which transcends all understanding, will guard your hearts and minds in Christ Jesus"* (Philippians 4:5-7 NIV).

Darkness of Depression

"Come quickly, Lord, and answer me, for my depression deepens. Don't turn away from me, or I will die" (Psalm 143:7 NLT). *"Why am I discouraged? Why so sad? I will put my hope in God! I will praise him again. . ."* (Psalm 5:5 NLT).

Are you suffering from depression, or do you know someone who is? If so, you realize full well the sense of worthlessness, helplessness, and hopelessness depression can bring. If you watch television, you are aware of the many commercials advertising drugs to help people overcome the devastating effects of depression. Depression seems to be an epidemic in our society and there are many approaches to treating this disorder.

I recognize that some suffer depression brought on by physical problems—chemical imbalances, etc. Those may require professional help. Obviously, I can't offer you help in this area, except to encourage you to seek the help you need.

However, I am convinced that many suffer feelings of depression brought on by a spiritual vacuum in their lives. Claiming to be a Christian will not necessarily fill that vacuum. Often we see depressed Christians. Why?

A while back, I read a short sermon in the Religion section of our local newspaper. It was entitled, "When Your Roots Don't Hit the Water." The message dealt with depression and the title was derived from John 7:38 NLT: *"If you are thirsty, come to me! If you believe in me, come and drink! For the Scriptures declare that rivers of living water will flow out from within."* Here Jesus uses the term "living water" to refer to the Holy Spirit who is always available to believers because He lives within us. It is the Holy Spirit who stands ready to fill every spiritual need we have if we are willing.

We can become discouraged, depressed, and worried about what the future may hold. Adverse circumstances can bring on feelings of depression and despair. But your Heavenly Father is faithful and will sustain you. All too often we find ourselves doubting that God is really in control and we are reluctant to trust Him completely to take care of us.

When God is given first place at the center-court of your life, you can be content and sleep in peace. This is because the roots of your being are being nourished in the never-ending living water of life—the Holy Spirit. Sometimes, when we realize that not every situation will turn out the way we wish, the best we can hope for is a sense of God's peace. When you feel depressed, read the Bible's accounts of God's goodness, and meditate on them.

Nov 29

Chuckle: *"I thought you were counting calories," Loris reminded her friend Karla as she consumed her second milkshake.*

"Oh, I am," said Karla. "So far today, I'm at 5,760."

Quote: *"Waste no more time arguing what a good man (person) should be; be one."* ~ Marcus Aurelius

A Worthy Example

"In the same way, encourage the young men to live wisely in all they do. And you yourself must be an example to them by doing good deeds, of every kind. Let everything you do reflect the integrity and seriousness of your teaching. Let your teaching be so correct that it can't be criticized. Then those who want to argue will be ashamed because they won't have anything bad to say about us" (Titus 2: 6b-8 HCSB).

Titus, a Greek convert through Paul's ministry, had become Paul's special representative to the house churches on the island of Crete. Paul's letter to Titus instructed him about his responsibilities as leader of the churches—how to do his job. Titus' instructions are very similar to those in 1 Timothy with its instructions to young Timothy and other church leaders. Although brief, Titus is an important link in the discipleship process of a young Christian growing into a leadership role in a church.

As I studied these verses, I concluded that all of Paul's instructions and admonitions to Titus can be boiled down to one word, "godliness." A lack of godliness by a Christian provides ammunition to the critics of Christianity. As a pastor, I often heard words like these from unsaved and unchurched people: "I'm as good as those people in your church—they are nothing but a bunch of hypocrites." Unfortunately, there is sometimes much truth in such accusations. However, when people find themselves living outside the will of God and practicing worldly standards of conduct, it's easy to denigrate someone else in order to make themselves look more virtuous.

Paul wanted Titus to be so righteous in both his living and his teaching that no one could find fault with either. Paul wanted Titus to be such a good example to those with whom he mingled that they might see the goodness in his life and strive to imitate him rather than find fault with him. What a wonderful goal for each of us as we yield to the Holy Spirit as our guide, teacher, and encourager. Even when we are not aware that we are being observed, many sets of skeptical eyes are likely to be upon us.

Blackmailers once sent C. H. Spurgeon a letter to the effect that if he did not place a certain amount of money in a certain place at a certain time, they would publish some things in the newspapers that would defame him and ruin his public ministry. Spurgeon left at the station a letter in reply: "You and your like are requested to publish all you know about me across the heavens." He knew his life was blameless in the eyes of men and therefore, they could not touch his character." ~ Illustrations for Biblical Preaching; Edited by Michael P. Green

I wonder how many of us would have the courage and confidence in our character and reputation to react as did C. H. Spurgeon?

Nov 30

Chuckle: *Can it be a mistake that "stressed" is "desserts" spelled backwards?*

Good Quote: *"If we have faith without works, or works without faith, we have washed the window on one side only."* ~ William Arthur Ward

Faith and Works

"The gentiles have been made right with God by faith, even though they were not seeking him. But the Jews, who tried so hard to get right with God by keeping the law, never succeeded. Why not? Because they were trying to get right with God by keeping the law and being good instead of depending on faith" (Romans 9:30-32 NLT).

What a difference it would make in our world if everyone understood the letter, the spirit, and the implications of this passage. There is a deep-seated conviction in the minds of many that goodness (righteousness) is measured by what we do—the good things we accomplish in this life.

We continue to think we must impress God by our good deeds/works to earn His acceptance and approval so we can be assured a place in His heavenly presence. This salvation by works idea blinds people to the blessed truth that it is the righteousness of Jesus, not ours, that reconciles us to God. Believing that we must earn God's approval serves as a stumbling block to attaining true righteousness through faith.

The only righteousness that makes us acceptable in God's sight is the righteousness imputed to us by Jesus Christ, and this righteousness only becomes our own through faith in Him. We may think that attending church, doing church work, giving offerings, and being nice to people will be enough to earn God's favor. Paul tells us the approach will never succeed.

We can only be saved by putting our faith in Jesus Christ and what He has done on the cross at Calvary. *"God saved you by his special favor (grace) when you believed. And you can't take credit for this: it is a gift of God. Salvation is not a reward for the good things we have done, so none of us can boast about it"* (Ephesians 2:8-9 NLT).

If salvation is only through faith in Jesus Christ, what place does good deeds have in our lives? It's really quite simple. Good deeds that please God are those done for His glory as a result of our relationship to Him through Christ, not to earn that relationship. *"For we are God's masterpiece. He has created us anew in Christ Jesus, so that we can do the good things (works) he planned for us long ago"* (Ephesians 2:10 NLT).

Our salvation is something only God can do through His creative power at work in us. We become Christians through God's grace (unmerited favor), not as the result of our own efforts, abilities, or acts of service. God's intention is that our salvation will result in acts of service. We work for Him out of love and gratitude because we have been saved, not to be saved.

Dec 01

Chuckle: *A man was looking at himself in a mirror. He said, "I look horrible, I feel fat and ugly. Please pay me a compliment." The wife said, "Your eyesight is near perfect!"*

Quote: *"Spiritual growth involves a constantly changing conception of a changeless God."* ~ William Arthur Ward

It Runs in the Family

"Whoever does God's will is my brother and sister and mother" (Mark 3:35 NLT). *"Listen to your father, who gave you life"* (Proverbs 23:22 NIV). *"Honor your father and mother—which is the first commandment with a promise"* (Ephesians 6:2 NIV).

On several occasions, I have been told that my son's voice sounds like mine, especially during telephone conversations. How often have you observed that someone walks, talks, acts, or looks like his or her parents? We call these characteristics family traits, and we sometimes hear words like, "it runs in the family." We all are aware that the DNA of our parents, grandparents, and more distant ancestors determines our physical characteristics and their influence on our lives determines how we sound and how we act.

In our passage, Jesus says if we do the will of God, we are His family. In Ephesians 2:19, we are told that we are *"members of God's household."* If we are members of His family, our lives will reflect the traits of Jesus—we will become like Him. People will be reminded of Him when they see or hear us. I'm reminded of the words of the apostle Paul: *"Your attitude (mind) should be the same as that of Christ Jesus"* (Philippians 2:5 NIV). It is our attitude/mind that determines how we talk and act. It is God's will that we become more and more like Jesus each day and exhibit the family traits that we see in Him.

When Jesus was here on earth, He walked daily in close communion with and submission to His Father. When we do the same things, we share a family trait with Jesus as His brothers and sisters. The Bible tells us that we should *"be imitators of God, therefore, as dearly loved children and live a life of love, just as Christ loved us and gave himself up for us as a fragrant offering and sacrifice to God"* (Ephesians 5:1-2NIV). Our voices and our actions should be modeled after those of our Lord Himself.

Just as children imitate their parents who love them, it should be our desire to imitate our Lord. His great love caused Him to sacrifice Himself for you and me so that we might live. Our love for others should be just like Jesus' love for us—a love that goes far beyond affection to self-sacrificing service. This kind of love should be a spiritual family trait in the family of Christ. It should run in our family.

"Therefore, as we have opportunity, let us do good to all people, especially to those who belong to the family of believers" (Galatians 6:10 NIV).

Dec 02

Chuckle: *"Do you believe in life after death?" the boss asked his employee.*

"Yes, of course sir."

"Well then, that makes everything just fine," the boss went on. "After you left early yesterday to go to your grandmother's funeral, she stopped by to see you!"

Quote: *"Oh, the comfort, the inexpressible comfort, of feeling safe with a person, having neither to weigh thoughts nor measure words, but to pour them all out just as they are, chaff and grain together, knowing that a hand of a faithful friend will take and sift them, keep what is worth keeping, and then, with a breath of kindness blow the rest away."* ~ George Elliott (Marian Evans Cross).

Friends Build Us Up

"As iron sharpens iron, so a man sharpens the countenance of his friend" (Proverbs 27:17 TAB).

Here are some qualities, with related Scriptures, that describe Christian friendships based on respect, brotherly love, and friendship love:

Friends trust each other. A friend can be trusted to keep to themselves what you have shared in confidence. *"A gossip betrays a confidence, but a trustworthy man (person) keeps a secret"* (Proverbs 11:13 NIV).

Friends feel safe with each other. You can be yourself. There is no need for pretenses. *"Be kind and compassionate to one another, forgiving each other, just as in Christ God forgave you"* (Ephesians 4:32 NIV).

Friends are honest with each other. The friend who sees

the other going down a dangerous path will not hesitate to sound a loving but firm warning. *"Wounds from a friend can be trusted, but an enemy multiplies kisses"* (Proverbs 27:6 NIV).

Friends freely share with each other. This includes fears, anxieties, burdens, insecurities, and questions. *"Carry each other's burdens, and in this way you will fulfill the law of Christ"* (Galatians 6:2 NIV).

Friends enjoy mutual acceptance—even with all their faults. *"Accept one another, then, just as Christ accepted you, in order to bring praise to God"* (Romans 15:7 NIV).

Friends accept responsibility for the relationship. They will not allow it to deteriorate even after heated disagreements. They will not rest until the air is cleared and the relationship completely restored. *"First go and be reconciled to your brother; then come and offer your gift"* (Matthew 5:24b NIV).

Friends are encouragers, not fault-finders. They build each other up, not tear each other down. *"But encourage one another daily, as long as it is called Today, so that none of you may be hardened by sin's deceitfulness"* (Hebrews 3:13 NIV).

True friends are faithful prayer partners. They are strong and effective intercessors on behalf of their friends. *". . . The prayer of a righteous man is powerful and effective"* (James 5:16 NIV).

A true friend is one of the greatest gifts a person can receive.

Dec03

Chuckle: *The prospective father-in-law asked, "Young man, can you support a family?"*

The surprised groom-to-be replied, "Well, mmm, No. I was just planning to support your daughter. The rest of you will have to fend for yourselves!"

Quote: *"When a friend laughs, it is for him to disclose the subject of his joy; when he weeps, it is for me to discover the cause of his sorrow."* ~ Joseph Francois Desmahis

Friends Always Love

"A friend loves at all times, and is born, as a brother (or sister), for adversity" (Proverbs 17:17 TAB). *"The man of many friends (a friend of all the world) will prove himself a bad friend, but there is a friend that sticks closer than a brother"* (Proverbs 18:24 TAB).

In these verses we see that true friends love us like brothers or sisters and are essential to our well-being, especially during times of adversity. There is also a warning about making friends with the world. .

According to the dictionary, a friend is *"A person whom one knows well and likes; a person on the same side in a struggle—an ally."* Another definition: *"A friend is the first person who comes in when the whole world has gone out."* People need the strength of a few solid relationships rather than a large number of superficial ones. Trying to make friends with "bad company" can bring pain and disappointment. To better understand friendship from a Biblical perspective, let's think of some other human interactions that are valuable and necessary, but are not genuine friendships.

Jesus loved all people but related to them on various levels.

He preached to some, He ministered to the individual spiritual needs of some, and He even performed miracles of physical healing for others. But He related in a different way to His twelve disciples. The closeness He enjoyed with them was unique, and even among the Twelve, there were three whom Jesus seemed to relate to more closely as friends. "*. . . Jesus took Peter, James, and John with him and led them up a high mountain, where they were alone. There he was transfigured before them*" (See Mark 9:2).

You can put yourself through a lot of anguish and heartache if you try to be friends with everyone, because not every relationship will reach the level of friendship love. However, this is not to say that other human interactions are not healthy, nor should they be avoided—just the opposite. When you see a person in need and you reach out to him or her in ministry, you have shown obedience to our Lord by showing love, compassion, and caring. But the needy person may never be your close friend.

On the other hand, when you have a true friend, the two of you will give to each other in an equal and unselfish way. Both will be strengthened, blessed, and comforted by the relationship.

In our Christian lives, we can identify three types of relationships. (1) First, there are those to whom we need to minister in their time of need, but they may give little or nothing to us in return. Our joy comes from helping people, not receiving. (2) Second, there are those we need to minister to us in our times of need, but we may return little or nothing to them. (3) A third kind of relationship is true friendship. This special relationship reflects mutual love, respect, kindness, sharing, and never-ending loyalty.

Dec 04

Chuckle: *"What papers do I need for my trip to England?" a college student asked the travel agent.*

"A passport and a visa," was the reply.

"I already have the passport, but . . . do you think they'd accept MasterCard?"

Quote: *"A real friend is the one who will tell you of your faults and follies in prosperity and assist with his hand and heart in adversity."* ~ Unknown Source

Honoring a Friend

Mephibosheth knelt down again and said (to King David), "Why should you care about me?" (2 Samuel 9:8 CEV).

One of the most beautiful stories of love and friendship recorded in the Bible involves the friendship between King David and King Saul's son, Jonathan. Their friendship was steadfast even through the most difficult of circumstances.

After Jonathan had been killed in battle, David's concern shifted to Jonathan's family and he sought ways to honor Jonathan's memory by bestowing kindness on his descendants. The only one he could find was a son, Mephibosheth, who was crippled from infancy.

When called before the King, Mephibosheth could not believe or understand why the great King should care about him and show such kindness. But because of his love for his friend, David warmly welcomed Mephibosheth into his home and cared for him. This was David's way of honoring his friend. The unconditional love David had for Jonathon was transferred to Mephibosheth, who could not understand why David should care about him.

As I read this beautiful story, I was reminded how unworthy I am to be the recipient of God's unconditional love as demonstrated by the sacrifice of Jesus for my sins. *"But God demonstrated his own love for us in this: While we were still sinners, Christ died for us"* (Romans 5:8 NIV). The psalmist questioned why God should care about mankind. *"When I consider your heavens, the work of your fingers, the moon and the stars, which you have set in place, what is man that you are mindful of him, . . .?"* (Psalm 8:3-4 NIV).

No matter how insignificant, unworthy, or unlovable you may feel, any fears you may have regarding God's love for you are unfounded. God has extended you a lasting invitation to come into His presence with assurance and experience His unconditional love through faith in Jesus Christ.

Do you have a precious friend to whom you are deeply indebted for his or her unconditional love, kindness, encouragement, and faithfulness? This story about David, Jonathan, and Mephibosheth should challenge us to examine our friendships and our responsibilities to them and their families. Friendships should never be taken for granted. They must be cherished, nourished, and nurtured if they are to become true friendships.

Dec 05

Chuckle: A little boys prayer: *"Dear God, please take care of my daddy and mommy and my sister and my brother and my doggy and me. Oh, please take care of yourself, God. If anything happens to you, we're gonna be in a big mess!"*

Quote: *"The love of God is like the Amazon River flowing down to water a single daisy."* ~ Unknown Source

God Cares for You

"Give all your worries and cares to God, for he cares about what happens to you" (1 Peter 5:7 NLT).

The Christmas season is a time of happiness, rejoicing, and excitement for many; but for others it is a time of loneliness, worry, anxiety, stress, and even fear. You may have lost a loved one this year and this will be your first Christmas without him or her. You may have lost your job and are suffering through difficult times financially. You may be worried about not having money to buy gifts for those you love. You may be suffering with health issues and are fearful of what the future holds. Any of these unpleasant conditions can cause you to withdraw from those who love you and to feel sorry for yourself. You may be tempted to wallow in self-pity.

Before you let yourself slip into the pits emotionally, stop for a moment and reflect on the goodness of the God we serve. *"Give your worries to the Lord, and he will take care of you. He will never let good people down"* (Psalm 55:22 NCV). Claim God's promises and let go of those debilitating fears and anxieties. If you insist in holding on to your worries, they will prevent you from enjoying the life and blessings God has given you. Like the old hymn says: *"Take your burdens to the Lord and leave them there."*

Rejoice because God loves you and is genuinely concerned about what's going on in your life. Others may fail you, but God will not. Don't submit yourself to circumstances but to the Lord who controls circumstances. He specializes in helping you deal with even the most severe difficulties and can give you His joy as He carries those burdens for you. Claim and believe God's promise that He loves you and will take care of you.

Two young girls were talking, and one said she had ten pennies. The other girl looked into her hand and only saw five.

She said, "you only have five pennies."

The first girl replied, "I have five and my father told me he would give me five more tonight. So I have ten." She understood that her father's promise was as good as done.

Regardless of your circumstances this Christmas, just remember that God loves you greatly and wants to carry your burdens for you. Your Father's promises are trustworthy and as good as kept.

Dec 06

Chuckle: *When my grandson asked me how old I was, I teasingly replied, "I'm not sure."*

"Look in your underwear, Grandpa," he advised. "mine says I'm four to six."

Quote: *"The visible marks of extraordinary wisdom and power appear so plainly in all the works of creation that a rational creature who will but seriously reflect on them cannot miss the discovery of the Deity."* ~ John Loche

God's Masterpiece

"If anyone is in Christ, he is a new creation; the old is gone, the new has come!" (2 Corinthians 5:17 NIV). *"For we are God's masterpiece. He has created us anew in Christ Jesus, so that we can do the good things he planned for us long ago"* (Ephesians 2:10 NLT).

The Greek word translated as "masterpiece" is the same word translated as "poem." In its broadest meaning, it describes God's poem, work of art, workmanship—His perfect masterpiece. When we fully grasp the significance of this miracle God performs in our lives, our love and appreciation for Him will know no bounds.

Have you ever thought of yourself as God's crowning, creative act? We all share in being the crown jewel of His physical creation, and when we are created anew in Christ, we become God's ultimate and crowning, creative work—the people God intended us to be from the beginning. We are made new from the inside out by the Holy Spirit working in us.

Do you fully understand how important you are to God, and what He has done for you through Jesus Christ? Our salvation is something that only God can accomplish; and as He does His creative work in us, we become His spiritual masterpiece.

Many places in Scripture we are told that it is because of God's great love that Christ died to pay the penalty for our sins. By God's grace, through faith in Jesus Christ, we are saved and created anew for God's purpose. As God's "new creation," the good things we do allow God's grace to flow through us and into the lives of others and display His creative handiwork to the world. Our transformation from a life of selfish and sinful self-centeredness to a life of Christ-likeness—in both our words and actions—bears witness to the love and power of our heavenly Father.

It's true that no action or work can help us attain salvation, but it is also true that God intends for our salvation (new creation) to result in selfless acts of service. In other words, we cannot be saved by doing good things, but we are saved to do good things which bless others and honor and glorify our Lord. We are saved for a purpose. Let's demonstrate the love of Christ so faithfully that everyone will know we are God's new creation in Christ Jesus—His creative masterpiece.

Dec 07

Chuckle: *"How come wrong numbers are never busy?"*

Good Quote: *"The way we pray shows how we live; the way we live shows how we pray."* ~ William Arthur Ward

God's Perfect Timing

"For you know quite well that the day of the Lord will come unexpectedly, like a thief in the night" (1 Thessalonians 5:2 NLT).

In chapter four, Paul described the events of Jesus return to remove His church (all believers) from the earth. Here in chapter five, he deals with the timing of our Lord's return. How and when Jesus Christ will return was an often asked question in Paul's time, as it is now. Most of us live by the clock and are constantly looking at our watches and calendars as we anticipate our next church service, meeting, work assignment, or vacation. I must admit I am a stickler for things being done on time and according to plan.

When thinking about the return of our Lord, we must remember that we aren't God and we do not view time from His perspective. Of course God knows all about time. After all, He created it. But God's time-table is difficult for us to understand. For us to try to predict with certainty the date for Christ's return is an exercise in futility and foolishness. It is not for us to know these things. Jesus Said, *"No one knows about that day or hour, not even the angels in heaven, nor the Son, but only the Father"* (Matthew 24:36 NIV). Evidently, the timing of Christ's return is a closely guarded secret even within the Godhead. All we know is that the event is certain to happen.

The key message from Paul's writings and the words of Jesus is that we cannot know when Christ will return, but we should be ready for Him to return at any moment. There's no way that God will adjust His time-table just to suit us. God's timing is always perfect and everything fits into His master plan for the universe, the earth, and His children. If we understood all about God's timing, we would be God.

Many have been made to look foolish by predicting exact dates for Christ's return. None of their predictions have been correct. Having said this, we do know from Scripture that many of the prophecies have been fulfilled that are prerequisites to our Lord's return, and this has led many of us to believe His return could be soon. But we just can't know for certain. As Christians, we should just trust God and His perfect timing, be ready, continue our work for Him, and listen for the trumpet call (See 1 Thessalonians 4:16).

Dec 08

Chuckle: *Eddie's father called up to him, "Eddie, if you don't stop playing that trumpet I think I will go crazy!"*

Eddie replied, "I think you have already, I stopped playing half an hour ago."

Quote: *"I was kept fast bound, not with exterior chains or irons, but with my own iron will. The enemy held my will and of it he had made a chain which fettered me fast."* ~ St. Augustine of Hippo

God's Will for You

Jesus prayed, *"Father, if you are willing, please remove this cup of suffering away from me. Yet I want your will, not mine"* (Luke 22:42 NLT). *"Why, you do not even know what will happen tomorrow... Instead, you ought to say, 'If it is the Lord's will, we will live and do this or that'"* (James 4:14-15 NIV).

As we awake each morning and begin to consider the day ahead, I wonder how many of us think to pray for God's will to be done today. As Christians, there are basically three attitudes with which we can meet a new day. We can (1) make our plans for the day and then ask God to bless the plans we have made; (2) pray for God to reveal His will and plans for our day with the assurance that He will give us strength and understanding to carry out those plans; or (3) ignore God's will and leave Him out of our daily planning altogether.

I've heard somewhere that if you want to make God laugh just tell Him of your plans. Our James passage makes it clear that to make plans without considering and seeking God's will beforehand is a dangerous practice. I'm sad to say, this is a trap that I have fallen into many times in my Christian life. The moment we decide to leave God out of our thoughts, plans, and prayers we are not walking with Him and seeking His will as He desires.

Romans 12:2 NLT gives us a formula for knowing and living out God's will. *"Don't copy the behavior and customs of this world, but let God transform you into a new person by changing the way you think. Then you will know what God wants you to do, and you will know how good and pleasing and perfect his will really is."* God has plans for His children that are good, pleasing, and perfect. But to ascertain God's will in all things requires a transformation of our hearts and minds by His Spirit.

We know that God only wants what is best for us and He proved this by giving His only Son to make a transformed life possible. If you have accepted God's free gift of eternal salvation through faith in Jesus Christ, won't you let God transform you into a totally new person by changing the way you think?

Then, like Jesus, your primary goal in life will be to know and live by God's will for your life. Agreeing with God in all circumstances will result in a more satisfying and happy life.

Remember this old hymn? *"Have thine own way, Lord! Have thine own way! Thou art the Potter, I am the clay. Mold me and make me After thy will, While I am waiting, Yielded and still."*

Dec 09

Chuckle: *After a service, a woman shook the pastor's hand and said, "I don't think I'll come back. Every time I come, you sing either 'He Arose' or 'Silent Night.'"*

Good Quote: *"Grumbling and gratitude are, for the child of God, in conflict."* ~ Billy Graham

Grumbling or Gratitude

"I know what it is to be in need, and I know what it is to have plenty. I have learned the secret of being content in any and every situation, whether well fed or hungry, whether living in plenty or in want. I can do everything through him who gives me strength" (Philippians 4:12-13 NIV).

In his book, "Storm Warning," Billy Graham makes this statement: *"Be grateful and you won't grumble—grumble and you won't be grateful."* These words caused me to think about their implications for Christian living. I have found that often many of us Christians allow our appreciation for what God has done for us to diminish and instead, we concentrate on what we don't have and what He hasn't done for us. This attitude is not new to God's people.

You will remember how God rescued the Israelite slaves from bondage in Egypt and began to lead them toward the Promised Land. Initially, they were excited about their relationship to God and deeply grateful for His goodness and favor He had shown them. However, as they trekked across the desert, it wasn't long until they forgot what God had done for them and began to grumble and complain. Their hearts were no longer filled with gratitude because they no longer had a passion for God. They were no longer grateful. How quickly we can forget God's goodness.

Perhaps you have allowed difficulties in your life to cause you to forget what God has done for you. Perhaps you have forgotten His great love shown when you received His salvation through faith in Jesus Christ. Maybe His indwelling Holy Spirit has become a ho-hum reality which you take for granted. You may be grumbling because you have less of this world's possessions than someone else or you're experiencing a rough patch in life. Instead of feeling close to God and grateful for His love, grace, and mercies, you may feel like grumbling.

Like the apostle Paul expressed in our text, God wants us to be content with our station in life. But more than that, He wants us to walk so close to Him that we will understand what He is trying to teach us by not giving us everything we want when we want it. He wants us to have a passion for Him that results in our knowing, trusting, and obeying Him.

However, if our passion for Him is allowed to cool, we will begin grumbling about everything. Like Paul, you should know God wants to give you the strength to do everything He wants you to do.

Let's praise Him with gratitude and avoid grumbling.

Dec 10

Chuckle: Child's Prayer: *"Dear God, we read that Thomas Edison made light. But in Sunday School they said you did it. So I bet he stoled your idea." Sincerely, Donna*

Quote: "Think of all the beauty still left around you and be happy." ~ Anne Frank

A Happy Face Reveals Your Heart

"A cheerful look brings joy to the heart; good news makes for good health" (Proverbs 15:30 NLT). *"A twinkle in the eye means joy in the heart, and good news makes you feel fit as a fiddle"* (MSG).

When I stopped for a sandwich at a local SUBWAY store sometime back, the place was humming with a long line of customers waiting to be served. Behind the counter was an attractive middle-aged lady with the most pleasant face I had seen in some time. Her radiant smile, patience, and kind words lifted the spirits of those standing in line. She appeared totally happy and content as she rushed to fill the rapid-fire orders from hungry customers. She made the whole experience one I will not soon forget. I thought at the time, that's the demeanor each and every Christian should project.

Can others perceive that you are a Christian by just looking at you? Does your countenance reveal the joy in your heart? Do your words and actions reflect the love of Christ to those around you? If you are living with an attitude of praise and thanksgiving to God, your actions will show it. You know you are not alone as you walk through even the most difficult times of your life and that confidence in Gods never-ending presence fills you with feelings of joy, contentment, peace, and excitement that cannot be hidden.

When others see joy in your life, no doubt it will bring joy to theirs. Jesus said, *"By this all men will know you are my disciples if you love one another"* (John 13:35). A person experiencing the real joy of Jesus Christ will love others and want to share that joy. As you show that love, and others see you doing it, you are a living testimony of what Christ has done for you.

As the "good news" (gospel) of Jesus Christ brings joy to your heart and transforms your life, that same good news will bring the same results to others. Good news is always a tonic for the body and soul. People will know by your expressions of love and happy face that you are living in fellowship with God.

Dec 11

Chuckle: *"Life is an endless struggle full of frustrations and challenges, but eventually you find a hairstylist you like."*

Quote: *"Blessed are those who can give without remembering, and take without forgetting."* ~ Elizabeth Bibesco

Hard Times and New Opportunities

"As a result, it has become clear throughout the whole palace guard and to everyone else that I am in chains for Christ. Because of my chains, most of the brothers in the Lord have been encouraged to speak the word of God more courageously and fearlessly" (Philippians 1:13-14 NIV).

Adversities bring new opportunities to share Christ. It is in times of trouble that our true Christianity becomes evident—when our faith measures up to the test. Difficulties make evident our faith, which should set us apart from those without Christ. Paul wrote in Romans 15:20, *"It has always been my ambition to preach the gospel where Christ was not known."* His arrest and imprisonment, to keep him from his mission, actually afforded him opportunity to continue it.

While he was in prison in Rome, *"boldly and without hindrance he preached the kingdom of God and taught about Jesus Christ"* (Acts 28:31). In Philippians 4:22, we can see how effective Paul was in spreading the gospel message. *"All the saints greet you, especially those who belong to Caesar's household."*

Often, while dealing with our own adversities, God provides opportunities to share the gospel with others. This truth was recently brought home to me in a personal way.

While being treated for my own health problem, I was

afforded the opportunity to witness and minister to a physician who is dealing with advanced cancer.

Adversities bring new opportunities to encourage others. *"Because of my chains, most of the brothers in the Lord have been encouraged to speak the word of God more courageously and fearlessly"* (Philippians 1:14). I'm reminded of Peter and John, who had been threatened and warned by the religious rulers to stop preaching in the name of Jesus. They boldly said to them, *"Judge for yourselves whether it is right in God's sight to obey you rather than God. For we cannot help speaking about what we have seen and heard"* (Acts 4:19).

Christians enduring hard times can serve as role models for less mature believers. Paul's imprisonment served as a catalyst for Roman believers to spring into action for the Lord. If he could continue preaching while in chains, surely they could do it in their circumstances. In a time when persecution of Christians was increasing, the church at Rome was in dire need of encouragement. Paul's trouble and ensuing testimony gave them such encouragement.

Could it be that your faithfulness to God during difficult times would serve as an encouragement for others to serve the Lord more faithfully?

Someone has said, *"A brook would lose its song if God removed all the rocks."*

Dec 12

Chuckle: *"I finally got my head together, and then my body fell apart!"*

Ponder This: *"Hate at its best will distort you; at its worst it will destroy you, but it will always immobilize you."* ~ Alex Haley, author of "Roots."

Harboring Hatred Is Harmful

"Anyone who hates another Christian is really a murderer at heart" (1 John 3:15 NLT). *"Hatred stirs up dissension, but love covers over all wrongs"* (Proverbs 10:12 NIV).

"Hatred" is defined as a strong dislike for someone. Is there anyone you just can't stand? Is there a burning rage against someone smoldering deep within your heart? If you find yourself answering "yes" to these questions, I don't need to remind you of the misery that such feelings can bring into your life. It takes a lot of energy and effort to harbor hatred because hatred is a terribly destructive force and will eventually consume you.

There is no doubt that Christians are to love all people but despise sin. In our 1 John passage, John echoes Jesus' teaching that whoever hates another person is a murderer at heart (Matthew 5:21, 22).

Christianity is a religion of the heart and outward compliance with a set of standards alone is not enough. It is the condition of the heart that matters to God. *"Man looks at the outward appearance, but the Lord looks at the heart"* (1 Samuel 16:7 NIV). Bitterness against someone who has wronged you is an evil cancer within you that can render you useless as a Christian.

I think the best test to determine if you are harboring hatred toward someone is to answer this question: Do you find yourself hoping that a person will get what's coming to him or her—that something bad will happen to him or her?

If you consciously wish hardship on anyone, you are exercising your hatred. If someone has committed a sinful offense against you, it is alright to hate their sin, but not the person. Your reaction should be to ask God to help you love the offender by enabling you to pray for that person. Remember how Jesus looked down from the cross at His tormentors and said, *"Father, forgive them, for they do not know what they are doing"* (Luke 23:34 NIV). Jesus never stopped loving—no matter the offense.

Hatred comes from being concerned for yourself at the expense of others. Instead, allow the Holy Spirit to fill and control your life, leaving no room for hatred and bitterness. Anger leads to bitterness then to hatred. Love, mercy, forgiveness, and humility are powerful weapons against hatred. *"Get rid of all bitterness. . . . Instead, be kind to each other, tenderhearted, forgiving one another"* (Ephesians 4:31-32 NNLT).

Here is the clincher. *"If anyone says, 'I love God,' but hates a Christian brother or sister, that person is a liar; for if we don't love people we can see, how can we love God, whom we have not seen? And God himself has commanded that we must love not only him but our Christian brothers and sisters too"* (1 John 4:19b-21 NLT). God's love is the source of human love, and His kind of love is contagious.

If you love as God (Jesus) loves you, there will be no room in your heart for hatred.

Dec 13

Chuckle: *"A successful diet is the triumph of mind over platter."*

Quote: *"When you arise in the morning, think of what a precious privilege it is to be alive—to breathe, to think, to enjoy, to love."* ~ Marcus Aurelius

Taking Care of Our Bodies

"Do you not know that your body is a temple of the Holy Spirit, who is in you, whom you have received from God? You are not your own; you were bought at a price. Therefore, honor God with your body" (1 Corinthians 6:19-20 NIV).

According to the CDC, two major health problems in the United States are growing and growing rapidly—obesity and diabetes. There are exceptions of course, but the rapid increase in these two conditions is largely the result of unhealthy lifestyles including over-eating and lack of exercise. The CDC estimates that 70 percent of Americans are overweight or obese.

In our society, I'm afraid eating has become an end unto itself for many of us rather than a means to an end. Food should be the necessary fuel that keeps our bodies healthy and functioning properly. However, many of us eat for pleasure, not because we are really hungry but because we just like to eat. All too often we eat much more of the wrong foods than we need for health, work, and recreation. Getting people to adopt healthy diets and get more exercise are urgent challenges facing our society.

Let me tell you a success story from a few years back. The CDC had declared Huntington, West Virginia the fattest city in the United States. The pastor of the nearby First Baptist Church of Kenova decided to preach a sermon on the physical and spiritual dangers of obesity, and that sermon began a process that resulted in the ABC hit mini-series, *Jamie Oliver's Food Revolution.* The series was released March 21, 2010.

The congregation received the pastor's message with enthusiasm, started several healthy eating and exercise programs, became the catalyst for healthier foods in their local schools; and their success has had an impact on our country and around the world through the television series. The pastor said, *"collectively our people have literally lost more than 2000 pounds (a ton) and feel much better spiritually and physically."*

Christians should have a special motivation for taking care of our bodies, which the Scripture says are temples of the Holy Spirit who resides within us. How can we serve and honor God when we are so overweight and out of shape that our activities for Him are severely curtailed?

Jesus said, *"Love the Lord your God with all your heart, soul, mind, and strength, and your neighbor as yourself."* Pastor Willis of First Baptist Church of Kenova said this, *"We cannot love God with all our strength if we do not take care of our bodies, nor can we love our neighbor with total effectiveness if we have perpetual self-induced health issues."*

There are many unhealthy activities that do harm to our bodies. If we indulge, each of us must decide if we are *"honoring God with our bodies."*

Dec 14

Chuckle: *"Mom said she became an octogenarian on her last birthday. She can do as she wishes with her life, but I hope she doesn't will them all her money!"*

Quote: *"Holiness includes what we call moral goodness but moral goodness is not the same as holiness. It is only a constituent part of it."* ~ Graham Leonard

Holy Living

"Since you have been raised to new life with Christ, set your sights on the realities of heaven, where Christ sits at God's right hand in the place of honor and power. Let heaven fill your thoughts. Do not think only about things down here on earth" (Colossians 3:1-2 NLT).

What a different world it would be if all who claim to be Christians truly focused on making our lives holy. In this chapter, we can learn what true Christian behavior should entail. Paul emphasizes the importance of allowing the Holy Spirit to change our moral and ethical standards and make us holy as God desires us to be. A right relationship with God will make us holy and result in right relationships with other believers.

A definition of "holy" includes: *"apartness, the separation of a person or thing from the common or profane for a divine use."* It also means to be reverent, pure, and chaste. To paraphrase, we are set apart by God for His service, and are to be pure in mind and spirit as we serve Him. *"But just as he who called us is holy, so be holy in all you do; for it is written: 'Be Holy, because I am holy'"* (1 Peter 1:15-16 NIV). Let's look at some prerequisites for holy living.

First: We must belong to God. *"Since you have been raised to new life with Christ."* We must belong to God by establishing a relationship with Him through faith in Jesus Christ. We can try our hardest to live good moral and benevolent lives, and many people may benefit from our kindness. But if we don't belong to God, it will all be in vain. Being good will not make us belong to God—and will not make us holy.

Second: If we belong to God, we are to *"set our sights on the realities of heaven . . and let heaven (things above) fill our thoughts."* Everything we do begins in our thoughts. If our thoughts are on the things of God, they will be reflected in the holy things we do. If we concentrate on the eternal rather than the temporal, it will show by the way we live and allow us to be holy as we live out God's purpose for us.

Third: If we belong to God, we will *"not think only about things down here on earth."* Sadly, our thoughts are not always completely pure and holy; and since God knows the thoughts and desires of our hearts, we can never meet God's standards for holy living while harboring sinful worldly thoughts and desires.

Howard Hendricks wisely observed, *"It is foolish to build a chicken coop on the foundation of a skyscraper."* The Christian who does not live a holy life is failing to utilize the foundation for his life that Christ has given him. When we are made holy, we will be *"useful to the Master and prepared to do any good work"* (2 Timothy 2:21 NIV).

Dec 15

Chuckle: *Ted: "You seem unhappy."*

Roger: "Yeah, I am. Living with my mother-in law has been stressful and hard on both me and my wife."

Ted: "Well, if it gets really bad, you could just ask her to move out."

Roger: "We can't. It's her house."

Quote: *"Gladly we desire to make other men perfect but we will not amend our own fault."* ~ Thomas à Kempis

Our Imperfections

"For all have sinned and fall short of the glory of God" (Romans 3:23 NIV). *"Stop judging others . . . First get rid of the log in your own eye; then perhaps you will see well enough to deal with the speck in your friend's eye"* (Matthew 7:5NLT).

Isn't it amazing how clearly we can see imperfections in others, but are totally blind when it comes to seeing our own? Many of us are really umpires at heart—we enjoy calling balls and strikes on someone else. But as we persist in judging others, we may come to view their minor imperfections as major, while seeing our own major faults as minor and insignificant.

Have you ever honestly taken stock of your imperfections? When you do, it may not be a very pleasant task. We all have blemishes and imperfections. For some, they are physical limitations. To others, they may be mental/emotional. Of course, our most serious imperfections are spiritual—originating from our propensity for sin.

By what standard should we measure our imperfections? This is the most important question we must answer if we are to honestly evaluate ourselves. The temptation is to say, "compared to others I know, I'm not so bad." However, comparing our imperfect lives to those of other imperfect people will not give us the answers we should desire. No, when we begin to measure our imperfections against God's standards, as spelled out in His Word, we are ready to let God's Holy Spirit convict us and give us the strength to deal with our imperfections—that is if we are truly repentant.

Our imperfections, from God's point of view, are called sins, even though we would prefer to call them missteps, mistakes, errors, shortcomings, etc. The most dangerous way to live with our imperfections is to become comfortable with them and go through life as if there is no need for alarm. The apostle Paul lived as close to perfection in his relationship with his Lord as any Christian who has ever lived. Yet, Paul was keenly aware of how far he was from spiritual maturity and perfection. Here's what he has to say:

"I don't mean to say that I have already achieved these things or that I have already reached perfection! But I keep working toward that day when I will finally be all that Christ Jesus saved me for and wants me to be" (Philippians 3:12 NLT).

Instead of finding imperfections in others, we are well served by turning our faults and imperfections over to God and letting Him deal with them. *"If we confess our sins, he is faithful and just and will forgive us our sins and purify us from all unrighteousness"* (1 John 1:9 NIV).

Dec 16

Chuckle: *"Detective: "How did you get into counterfeiting?"*
Criminal: "I answered an ad that said, 'Make money at home.'"

Quote: *"Your idol is shattered in the dust to prove that God's dust is greater than your idol."* ~ Rabindranath Tagore

Indulging in Idols

"So put to death the sinful, earthly things lurking within you. Have nothing to do with sexual sin, impurity, lust, and shameful desires. Don't be greedy for the good things of this life, for that is idolatry" (Colossians 3:5 NLT).

If I were to ask you if you worship idols, your initial response would likely be, "No, of course not!" But, after carefully digesting God's Word, we must come to understand that most of us likely have, or have had, idols in our lives. Let's think about this together.

When the apostle Paul was alive, idol worship was rampant. Perhaps the most revered idol was in the city of Ephesus—the goddess Diana. The huge statue was the centerpiece of a magnificent temple recognized as one of the major wonders of the world. In those days, many people made their livings from the manufacture of idols.

From our passage today we can readily see that anything that diverts our attention and devotion away from God can become an idol to us—making a god of earthly things. This can happen to us without our even being aware of what has happened. Our society today is perhaps even more idolatrous than in Paul's time. Instead of worshiping carved statues, we worship possessions, power, pleasures, or position as gods and pour our energies and financial resources into attaining such things.

You and I may say we have no idols and are placing God first in our lives. But Paul shows us some specific sins that can divert our attention away from God and become idols to us. He talks about earthly things lurking within us—our sinful nature. Many in our society are addicted to pornography, drugs, alcohol, gambling, etc. These can become the controlling forces over our lives and leave no room for allegiance to the true God. Paul specifically mentions greed as a sin of idolatry. Being greedy is wanting or taking all that one can get with no thought of what others need. It is the insatiable desire for what you don't have—making a god of gain.

Here Paul admonishes us to "put to death" all the sins produced by our earthly nature. If you are struggling with a sin that Paul points out in our passage, please be assured that God will grant you strength to overcome it in the power of His Spirit. The worst mistake we can make is to harbor some hidden sin while trying to portray the outward characteristics of a committed Christian—to live a lie. This will result in a feeling of terrible guilt and rob you of the joy God wants you to experience with Him.

If you know someone who is struggling with an idolatrous sin, please pray for that person and be an example to him or her by upholding Christ as most important in your life. Perhaps God will use you to help restore that person.

Dec 17

Chuckle: *A password audit found a young lady using this password: "MickeyMinniePlutoHueyLouieDeweyDonaldGoofySacramento." When asked why the long password, she said she was told that it had to be at least eight characters long and include at least one capital.*

Quote: *"Think of all the beauty still left around you and be happy."* ~ Anne Frank

Indelibly Marked

God said, *"I would not forget you! See, I have written your name on my hand"* (Isaiah 49:15-16 NLT).

The children of Israel were in bondage in Babylon. Some felt that God had forsaken and abandoned them. But Isaiah reminded them that God would never forget them, as a loving mother could never forget her little child. When God said He had written their names on His hand, He was referring to an ancient practice at the time of Isaiah's prophetic ministry. It was a custom to show their allegiance to some important person by permanently marking their hands with the name of that person.

In addition to God's marking the names of His people on His hand, there are numerous other references in Scripture that tell us God has placed our names in His permanent record if we know Jesus Christ as Savior and Lord. Our names are written in the Book of Life (Rev. 20:15; 21:27). Jesus *"calls his sheep (followers) by name"* (John 10:3 NIV). *"Having believed, you were marked in him with a seal, the promised Holy Spirit"* (Eph. 1:13 NIV). *"He (Jesus). . . set his seal of ownership on us . . ."*

(2 Cor. 1:22 NIV).

Like the children of Israel, there may be times when you feel God has forgotten you. But all these promises from God's Word, affirm that you belong to God and He has marked you as His most treasured possession—*"a people belonging to God"* (1 Pet. 2:9 NIV). God genuinely cares about you and you are always on His mind. I believe it was Max Lucado who said, *"If God carried a wallet, your picture would be in it."* There is ample evidence that God has committed to love and care for you, and there is not the remotest possibility that He will ever forget you or abandon you. *"God has said, 'Never will I leave you; never will I forsake you"* (Heb. 13:5 NIV).

If you have lost a loved one this year or some other tragedy has befallen you that makes you less than enthusiastic about celebrating Christmas, I pray you will draw comfort from knowing that God is aware of your pain and wants to grant you a special measure of His love, grace, and peace.

Please turn to Him and let Him fill your heart with His presence and His joy.

Dec 18

Chuckle: *The church custodian quit, and the pastor asked the organist if she would be able to clean the church. The organist thought before replying, "Do you mean that I now have to mind my keys and pews?"*

Quote: *"Control your thoughts and desires; they may break into words and actions at any moment."* ~ Unknown Source

What Influences You Most?

"But they delight in doing everything the Lord wants; day and night they think about his law" (Psalm 1:2 NLT).

Everything you watch, read, or listen to influences your life. If you watch, read, or listen to wholesome materials, you will be influenced in a positive way. The opposite is true as well. You may say: "I can watch trash on TV or read an off-color magazine or book without it affecting my thinking or the way I live." Let me explain why I believe this attitude to be wrong for Christians.

It's obvious that we have been influenced negatively by the things of the world if our actions become sinful. However, it may not be so obvious if only our thoughts are influenced. You can fool the people around you by playing the part of a faithful Christian while harboring sinful thoughts and desires. Failing to act on those secret desires does not mean you aren't sinning against God. Sins begin in our hearts and minds, but often don't remain there.

Remember, *"Men look on outward appearances, but God looks upon the heart"* (1 Samuel 16:7). *"For as he thinketh in his heart, so is he"* (Proverbs 23:7 KJV). *"As water reflects a face, so a man's heart reflects the man"* (Proverbs 27:19 NIV). Jesus said,

"But I tell you that anyone who looks at a woman lustfully has already committed adultery with her in his heart" (Matthew 5:28 NIV).

Our sinful thoughts may not result in outward rebellion against God, but they can keep us from doing anything worthwhile for Him. If our minds dwell on ungodly things, we become apathetic toward God's work and disinterested in spiritual things.

Here's a quick way to evaluate your heart and mind. Do you experience joy from studying God's Word and serving Him? If something else gives you greater joy, you have been influenced by the world.

Notice in our passage what makes devoted followers of God (Christ) happy—the Word of God. It occupies first place in their order of priorities. They think about it day and night. They fill their minds with the things important to God. If you meditate on the Bible and absorb the godly principles that nourish your heart, mind, and spirit you will find fulfillment and happiness that only God can give. You will not focus on temporal things that soon pass away, but upon the eternal that can never be taken from you.

Dec 19

Chuckle: How would you make a marriage work? *"Tell your wife that she looks pretty, even if she looks like a dump truck."* ~ Ricky, age 10

Quote: *"To God the Father, God the Son, And God the Spirit, Three in One, Be honour, praise, and glory given By all on earth, and all in heaven."* ~ Isaac Watts

Our Great Intercessor

"And the Holy Spirit helps us in our distress. For we don't know what we should pray for, nor how we should pray. But the Holy Spirit prays for us with groanings that cannot be expressed in words. And the Father who knows all hearts knows what the Spirit is saying, for the Spirit pleads for us believers in harmony with God's own will" (Romans 8:26-27 NLT).

Are there times when you feel so distressed, depressed, and discouraged that you don't know where to turn and have difficulty putting your feelings into words? Are there times when your feelings are so complex and confusing that you don't know how to ask God for relief? I'm sure each of us has experienced such feelings at one time or another. When this happens, we must be reminded that, as Christians, we are not alone in this battle of life. We are not limited by our own finite resources in coping with difficulties, disappointments, and distractions.

When you feel distressed it is not necessary to put your prayer requests into words because the Great Intercessor will do that for you. With God Himself helping you pray, there's never a reason to be hesitant or afraid to come to Him in prayer. *"Let us then approach the throne of grace with confidence (boldness), so that we may receive mercy and find grace to help us in our time of need"* (Hebrews 4:16 NIV).

We should boldly and confidently approach God even when we realize how little we know and how poorly equipped we are to pray properly. But the Holy Spirit stands ready to help us express our love for God, our deep desire to worship Him, our sincere attitude of repentance, and even our personal requests. Even when nothing but groans come from within us, the Holy Spirit understands and will intercede for us in accordance with God's own will—and God will certainly answer such prayers.

The Holy Spirit is God, but He is in some ways distinguishable from the Father. The Spirit prays for us to the Father. The Spirit is a form of God as is Jesus, the Son of God. This intercessory communications within the persons of the Godhead—Father, Son, and Holy Spirit—are a part of the great mystery of the Trinity.

The intercession of the Spirit introduces a level of divine communications which is far above the level of human words in which our sometimes awkward prayers are interpreted and translated into the high and majestic language of God Himself. PRAISE!!

Dec 20

Chuckle: *A new rural resident called the local authorities requesting the removal of the "Deer Crossing" sign on their road. Their reason was that many deer were being hit by cars and they no longer wanted them to cross there.*

Quote: *"Greatness is not found in possessions, power, position, or prestige. It is discovered in goodness, humility, service and character."* ~ William Arthur Ward

The Last Will Be First

Jesus said, *"But many who are first will be last, and many who are last will be first"* (Matthew 19:30 NIV).

You may remember the inspiring story of Derek Redmond, the sprinter who finished last in the 400 meter finals during the 1992 summer Olympics. He pulled a hamstring and only made it across the finish line with the help of his father who came out of the crowd to assist him. Derek garnered more attention and acclaim than the actual winner because of his courage and determination to finish the race and never quit. Even today, as we think about the scene, the runner who finished last is the first one we remember.

Jesus taught His disciples by saying, *". . . whoever wants to become great among you must be your servant, and whoever wants to be first must be your slave—just as the Son of Man did not come to be served, but to serve, and give his life as a ransom for many"* (Matthew 20:26-28 NIV).

You may feel as if you are always bringing up the rear—last place in the game of life. But it is a reality that most of us Christians will never receive the notoriety of a Billy Graham, Lottie Moon, or other well-known Christian faithful. We may never receive first place recognition in this life. However, it is not the world we seek to please, but the One who loves us and gave Himself for us. When it comes to being first or great, Jesus completely dismantled the world's values and turned them upside down, as reflected in the Beatitudes in Matthew 5. It is not our stature that will be rewarded but our enduring faithfulness—even for the small things we do for God's glory.

As we see in the above passage, our greatness and being first is dependent upon our humbling ourselves and being lowly servants to others. Jesus set the example for us as He came to serve and give His life for you and me. In this world, not many powerful and acclaimed people got to where they are by being humble, kind, and understanding. But in the heavenly world to come, the last will be first. We should not be working for human approval, but be faithful to the One whose approval really matters.

I started with a story about an Olympic 400 meter race. Listen to Paul's words to young Timothy as he thought about his eminent death. *"I have fought the good fight, I have finished the race, I have kept the faith. Now there is in store for me the crown of righteousness, which the Lord, the righteous Judge, will award to me on that day . . ."* (1 Timothy 4:7-8 NIV). Paul was not interested in being first in the eyes of the world, but in the eyes of his Lord. Paul was not alone as he finished his race. Like Derek Redmond, his Father was there to help him.

Dec 21

Chuckle: *Why did the bowlegged cowboy get fired? He couldn't keep his calves together!*

Quote: *"We may easily be too big for God to use, but never too small."* ~ D.L. Moody

Love As a Practice

"Serve one another in love" (Galatians 5:13 NIV).

Have you ever wondered why a physician's work is called a "practice?" I don't think any of us want a doctor "practicing" on us—we want him to attend to us only after he has perfected his skills. Of course we understand that in this case the word "practice" means he is applying his skills for the benefit of his patients. However, when it comes to Christian love, we need to practice it day in and day out in a life-long effort to get it right—to love as Jesus loves. *"Be imitators of God, therefore, as dearly loved children and live a life of love, just as Christ loved us and gave himself for us . . ."* (Ephesians 5:1-2 NIV).

Most Christians are pretty good at expressing their love to one another verbally or maybe even with a hug. Such expressions are rooted in warm and fuzzy feelings we have for our brothers and sisters in Christ. Telling others that we love them is a good thing and should never be neglected. But words alone just won't cut it when we apply the biblical standard to the way we should love one another.

Christian love is more than words and more than a warm emotional feeling. Christian love is serving the ones whom we love. It is demonstrated by our actions. It means getting our hands dirty as we help meet the needs of others. It means having the heart of a servant like our Lord who wrapped

Himself in a towel and washed the dusty or muddy feet of His disciples (See John 13:1-17).

Jesus set the bar extremely high for us when it comes to loving one another through acts of kindness and service. While none of us has reached the point where we can love like Jesus loves us, we must never stop striving to be like Him. Jesus said, *"As I have loved you, so you must love one another. By this all men will know that you are my disciples, if you love one another"* (John 13:34-35 NIV).

You know Lord how I serve you, with great emotional fervor, in the limelight. You know how eagerly I speak for you, at a women's club. You know how I effervesce when I promote a fellowship group. You know my genuine enthusiasm at a Bible study. But how would I react, I wonder, if you pointed to a basin of water, And asked me to wash the calloused feet of a bent and wrinkled old woman, day after day, month after month, In a room where nobody saw, and nobody knew?

~ Ruth Harms Calkin

Dec 22

Chuckle: *"Birthdays are good for you—the more you have, the longer you live!"*

Quote: *"Going to church doesn't make you a Christian any more than going to a garage makes you an automobile."* ~ William Ashley (Billy) Sunday

The Name You Bear

"The disciples were called Christians first at Antioch" (Acts 11:26 NIV).

The story is told about Alexander The Great, the great military leader of the fourth century B.C. He once confronted a cowardly soldier and asked him his name. The soldier replied, "Alexander." Then Alexander the Great said to him: "Change your ways or change your name."

Names are important even today and were especially so in biblical times. We bear the name "Christian" because of our relationship to Christ. But we must remember that being called "Christian" does not make us Christians. The story about Alexander the Great, caused me to wonder if my actions as a Christian would cause Jesus to say: "Change your ways or change your name."

Various names have been given to Christians that define them.

Believers: This term is used to describe the belief system of Christians. We believe—in God the Creator; the Bible, God's Holy Word; that we are sinners in need of a savior; that Jesus Christ is the Son of God and is our Savior because of His atoning sacrifice on Calvary's Cross; that Jesus arose from the dead on the third day; that we have been saved by God's grace through faith in Jesus Christ; that God's Holy Spirit lives within us; in the bodily return of Jesus Christ one day; and that eternity in heaven awaits all true Christians.

Disciples: This term means students, apprentices, and followers of Christ. A disciple is submissive to God as Jesus was submissive to the will of His Father when He died for the sins of the world. A disciple's actions are patterned after the life modelled by Jesus when He was here on earth. This includes living a life of love, humility, and service. Disciples strive to conform their lives to the will of Christ.

Saints: A biblical term describing all genuine Christians. Paul often began his writings with the words like: "To the saints in Christ Jesus at Philippi," etc. It means we have been sanctified (set apart) and made holy for God's service. It means we should live pure and holy lives, and live up to the name of Christ we bear.

Witnesses: Jesus said to His followers, *"You will receive power when the Holy Spirit comes on you; and you will be my witnesses in Jerusalem, and in Judea and Samaria, and to the ends of the earth"* (Acts 1:8 NIV). In New Testament times, faithful witnesses for Christ often laid down their lives as martyrs. When Peter and John were threatened for preaching in the name of Jesus, they said, *"Judge for yourselves whether it is right in God's sight to obey you rather than God. For we cannot help speaking about what we have seen and heard"* (Acts 4:19-20 NIV). We are charged by Jesus to tell others what we have experienced in Christ.

Are you and I living up to the name Christian?

Dec 23

Chuckle: *In Early America, it was not unusual for politicians to take advantage of a public hanging to address the crowd of spectators. On one occasion, the condemned man was told that a politician was going to speak, and he said, "Could you please hang me first?"*

Quote: *"Peace is more important than all justice: and peace was not made for the sake of justice, but justice for the sake of peace."* ~ Martin Luther

Peace Beyond Description

"I lay down and slept. I woke up in safety, for the LORD was watching over me. I am not afraid of ten thousand enemies who surround me on every side" (Psalm 3:5-6 NLT).

Real peace seems to be a rare commodity these days. The absence of peace is revealed by anxiety, fear, tenseness, and sleeplessness. Today, all sorts of medications are available just to help us get a good night's sleep. On the other hand, calmness, contentment, and joy are all indicators of an inward peace with God and those around you.

Are you troubled, anxious, or fretful this morning? Is peace something you yearn for but are not experiencing? If you answered "yes" to these questions, there is a tried and proven source of peace that the psalmist David had discovered—and you can discover as well.

Sleep does not come easily in a crisis and David was in a real crisis. His son Absalom had rebelled and gathered an army to defeat him and kill him. Yet, David was able to sleep peacefully even when surrounded by his enemies because he trusted in the Lord to whom he had committed his life.

If we truly commit our lives into God's hands and trust Him to see us through every circumstance, we too can have the peace that David had, even in the most troublesome times of our lives. Trust in God brings us peace from God. Also, the assurance of answered prayer brings peace.

If you are lying awake at night worrying and fretting about circumstances over which you have absolutely no control, pour out your heart to God, and thank Him that He is in complete control. Then peace and restful sleep will come.

"You will keep in perfect peace all who trust in you, all whose thoughts are fixed on you!" (Isaiah 26:3 NLT). We can never avoid strife in our world, but if we fix our thoughts on God through Scripture and prayer, we can have perfect peace even in times of turmoil. He can make us steady and stable and bring us rest even during our most severe crises. Christ is the only source of complete, lasting, and perfect peace.

Jesus said to His disciples: *"Peace I leave with you; my peace I give you. I do not give as the world gives. Do not let your hearts be troubled and do not be afraid"* (John 14:27 NIV).

Dec 24

Chuckle: *"A young preacher who was a guest preacher for a city church, in the absence of the pastor, prayed thusly for the pastor: 'May the pastor of this church be filled with fresh veal and zigor!"*

Quote: *"Nothing is so strong as gentleness and nothing is so gentle as real strength."* ~ Ralph W. Sockman

But You, O Bethlehem

"But you, O Bethlehem Ephrathah, are only a small village in Judah. Yet a ruler of Israel will come from you, one whose origins are from the distant past" (Micah 5:2 NLT).

Today we hear the prophetic voices from 700 B.C., foretelling not only the birth of Jesus, but the very village where He would be born. Ephrathah was the district in which Bethlehem was located. This is just one more tile in the mosaic of prophecy pointing to the day when God Himself, in the form of His Son, would enter our world as flesh and blood to live among us and identify with us.

The promised "ruler" is Jesus, the Messiah. The promised eternal King would be from the lineage of King David, who would come to live as a man. Bethlehem was also the place of David's birth and his ancestors lived there. *"This is a record of the ancestors of Jesus the Messiah, a descendant of King David and of Abraham"* (Matthew 1:1 NLT).

Jesus' existence can be traced to a time before the world was created. His eternal presence is revealed by the apostle John: *"In the beginning was the Word (Jesus), and the Word was with God, and the Word was God. He was with God in the beginning. Through him all things were made; without him nothing was made that has been made"* (John 1:1-3 NLT). Although eternal, Jesus Christ entered the stage of human history as the Christ Child, Jesus of Nazareth.

The prophecy of Micah helps us understand God's master plan for His Son to enter the world as a human being in the most humble of circumstances. Jesus made His entry into the world by being born in a stable to poverty-stricken parents in a small village called Bethlehem. There He was placed in an animal feed trough called a manger. This is the way God chose to send the King of Kings and Lord of Lords into this world to save us from the penalty of our sins and to give us the best life here on earth. Jesus said, *"I have come that you might have life, and have it to the full"* (John 10:10 NIV).

On this Christmas Eve, it is my prayer that you will experience the Spirit of Christmas in a new, fresh, and powerful way. May your heart be stirred when you reflect on the dimensions of God's love, grace, and mercy embodied in the Babe of Bethlehem whose birth we will celebrate tomorrow.

Dec 25

Chuckle: *If you turn on the lawn sprinklers on Christmas Eve to keep carolers away, you just might be a Scrooge.*

Amazing Quote: *"This will be a sign to you: You will find a baby wrapped in cloths and lying in a manger"* (Luke 2:12 NIV).

The Spirit of Christmas

"She will give birth to a son, and you are to give him the name Jesus, because he will save his people from their sins" (Matthew 1:21 NIV). *"All have sinned, and come short of the glory of God"* (Romans 3:23 NIV).

The spirit of Christmas is not about motifs, but redemption and salvation. If Christmas becomes only a time for decorations, shopping, and festivities, its significance will have been lost. Unfortunately, this seems to be the case across our land. Even those of us who are Christians are not immune to being caught up in a secular and commercialized Christmas. People often speak of the "spirit of Christmas" as if it is something to be caught while scurrying around in a shopping frenzy. You may have heard someone say, "I went shopping and caught the Christmas spirit." If tired feet, overspending, and standing in long lines constitute the Christmas spirit, we're all in trouble.

To me, the Christmas spirit is a warm feeling of love—being loved by God, loving others, and being loved by others. It's the spirit that says, "I want to give of myself to someone else." This kind of Christmas spirit comes from God. The real spirit of Christmas begins when we accept the best gift of all, the one born in a stable and laid in a feed trough, the one and only Son of the Most High God. When we accept His salvation and forgiveness, we receive the precious gift of His Holy Spirit who lives within us and guides our steps in this life.

In return for His amazing gift, God wants us to give ourselves to Him. To do this, we must be willing to abandon self and let God use us as He chooses. If Christ is born in our hearts, God is our Father, and the Holy Spirit is alive within us. Because of this truth, we will serve God by serving our brothers and sisters. As we experience the Spirit of Christmas, let's listen to the words of Jesus. *"Whoever wants to become great among you must be your servant; and whoever wants to be first must be your slave: even as the Son of Man did not come to be served, but to serve"* (Matt. 20:26-28 NIV).

If you want to receive the true Spirit of Christmas, you must be God's servant—by being the servant of others. Look again! *"But when the time had fully come, God sent his Son, born of woman, born under the law, to redeem those under law, that we might receive the full rights as sons. Because you are sons, God sent the Spirit of his Son, into our hearts"* (Gal. 4:4-6 NIV). God sent the Spirit of His Son into your heart, so that out of your heart you cry, *"My Father!"*

If the Christ of Christmas is only a nativity scene on your coffee table, He is not alive in you. If the star of Christmas is only an ornament on the Christmas tree, it has nothing to say.

But if the Christ of Christmas lives in your heart, He has a message for everyone to hear. The living Christ causes you to cry out in praise and thanksgiving!

Dec 26

Chuckle: *Sign in the window of a bank near a cemetery: "You can't take it with you when you go, but here's a chance to be near it!"*

Quote: *"Privilege and responsibility are two sides of the same coin."* ~ Unknown Source

Another Look at Jesus

"Your attitude should be the same as that of Christ Jesus: Who, being in the very nature God, did not consider equality with God something to be grasped, but made himself nothing, taking the very nature of a servant, being made in human likeness. And being found in appearance as a man humbled himself and became obedient to death—even death on a cross! Therefore, God exalted him (Jesus) to the highest place and gave him the name that is above every name, that at the name of Jesus every knee should bow, in heaven and on earth and under the earth, and every tongue confess that Jesus Christ is Lord, to the glory of God the Father" (Philippians 2:5-11 NIV).

What a beautiful word picture of who Jesus is and the example He has set for us when it comes to obedient living and humble service to God and to others. It reminds us one more time of the indescribable dimensions of His divine love for you and me.

"I marvel that whereas the ambitious dreams of myself, Caesar, and Alexander, should have vanished into thin air, a Judean peasant, Jesus, should be able to stretch His hands across the destinies of men and nations. I know men; and I tell you that Jesus Christ is no mere man. Between him and every other person in the world there is no possible term of comparison. Alexander,

Caesar, Charlemagne, and I myself have founded empires; but upon what do these creations of our genius depend? Upon force. Jesus alone founded his empire upon love; and to this very day millions would die for Him." ~ Attributed to Napoleon Bonaparte

The following is from an unknown source. The Lord Jesus Christ, whose birth we celebrate at Christmas, is not just a baby in a feed trough. He is not just a Judean carpenter. He is not just a great teacher. He is not just a character in a children's story. He is far more:

- The first time He came veiled as a child. The next time, He will be unveiled, and all the world will know and acknowledge who He is.
- The first time He came, a star marked His arrival. The next time, the heavens will roll up like a scroll, and the stars will fall out of the sky, and He Himself will light it.
- The first time He came, wise men and shepherds brought Him gifts. The next time, He will bring gifts and rewards for His own.
- The first time He came, there was no room for Him. The next time, the whole world will not be able to contain His glory.
- The first time He came, few attended His arrival. The next time everyone will see Him.
- The first time He came as a baby. Soon He will come and every knee shall bow, and every tongue confess that Jesus Christ is the sovereign Lord of Lords and King of Kings.

  We should marvel at these truths!

Dec 27

Chuckle: *A nurse was about to give a shot to a little girl. The girl screamed, "No! No! No!"*

"Lizzie, that's not polite behavior," her mother scolded.

Then the girl yelled even louder, "No thank you! No thank you, No thank you!"

Quote: *"Love is: Silence when your words would hurt; Patience when your neighbor's curt; Deafness when the scandal flows; Thoughtfulness for another's woes; Promptness when stern duty calls; Courage when misfortune falls."* ~ Unknown Source

Practice Makes Perfect

"May the Lord make your love for each other and for everyone else grow by leaps and bounds" (1 Thessalonians 3:12 CEV).

As long as I can remember I have heard the expression "practice makes perfect." More often than not it was used in reference to perfecting some physical skill, perhaps in sports or on the job. The more repetitions we do, the stronger and more skilled we become. The expression focuses on the need for hard work. Perhaps you've never thought about the need for practice or repetitions to become skilled at loving others. If we remember that the word "love" is an action word, not just a warm fuzzy emotional feeling, then the need for practice makes more sense.

When we Christians show love to others, we are giving expression to the love that God has shown us. *"If we love each other, God lives in us, and his love has been brought to full expression through us"* (1 John 4:12 NLT). If we allow the love of

God to fill our hearts and minds, it will overflow into the lives of others and reflect God's love for them. However, it's not enough just to show our love by being courteous and kind.

Our love must be shown by frequent and persistent acts of kindness that convincingly demonstrate our love in ways that mere words can never convey. God tells us He loves us (John 3:16), but He doesn't stop there. *"But God demonstrates his own love for us in this: while we were still sinners, Christ died for us"* (Romans 5:8 NIV). As we demonstrate our love to others over and over again, our ability to love should be growing with each repetition.

If you have become indifferent about showing God's love to others, or if your capacity to love has become stagnant and unchanged for a period of time, you can always ask God to refresh and refill you with His never-ending supply. Then actively and repetitively look for opportunities to practice loving in both words and deeds. *"Dear children, let us not love with words or tongue but with actions and truth"* (1 John 3:18 NIV). The more you practice loving as God loves you, the more proficient you will become and He will perfect His presence, power, and peace within you.

Dec 28

Chuckle: *A lady stopped for speeding was asked to show her driver's license. She replied, "Yesterday you took my license, now you expect me to show it to you!"*

Quote: *"For the Christian, praying should be like breathing. Just as breathing is the response of physical life to the presence of air, so prayer should be the response of spiritual life to the presence of God."* ~ Unknown Source

Prayer, Our Spiritual Breath

"Be joyful always; pray continually; give thanks in all circumstances, for this is God's will for you in Christ Jesus" (1 Thessalonians 5:16-17 NIV).

In the same way that we continually breathe physically, God would have us continually breathe spiritually through prayer. Prayer is not just a spiritual exercise, or keeping up appearances before others, or a shot in the dark—hoping God may hear. Prayer is conversing with your Heavenly Father in the same way you might talk with your earthly father. Your prayers are meant for His ears only and reveal the very essence of your being—the deepest recesses of your heart.

Our joyfulness, prayerfulness, and thankfulness should be continuous and should not ebb and flow with changing circumstances in our lives. You breathe physically through every situation, good or bad, and do not stop breathing when you have a physical crisis. And your oxygen flow becomes even more critical during difficult times. Likewise, we need spiritual breath at all times. Obeying the instructions in our passage—be joyful, keep on praying, and be thankful—often goes against our natural inclinations. However, when we make a conscious decision to do what God says in reference to prayer, we will find it much easier to be joyful and thankful.

Obviously, we cannot spend all our time on our knees in prayer, but it is possible for us to have a prayerful attitude at all times. It happens when your walk with the Lord becomes so close and intimate that you sense His presence with you every second of every day. His Holy Spirit's presence becomes an extension of your own—like you becoming one with Him. Once we reach this kind of relationship with God, it makes good sense that we converse with Him continually.

Prayer can become as normal as breathing when we acknowledge our dependence on God, realizing His presence within us, and determining to obey Him fully. Praying will then become natural, frequent, short, and spontaneous. One way to describe this concept is "breath prayers." As you think about your Lord during your daily activities, and as you breathe, you can use your inhalations as reminders to hear God speak to you and your exhalations as reminders to speak to God concerning the desires of your heart. For example, as you exhale, praise God for His boundless love and as you inhale, hear Him say, "I love you and am with you always." In other words your physical breathing can remind you to breathe spiritually.

One final thought: A continuous prayerful attitude should not replace regular times of prayer and meditation on God's Word, but be an outgrowth of regular times with God.

Dec 29

Chuckle: *"If all the people who sleep in church were laid end to end—they'd be a lot more comfortable!"*

Quote: *"Intercession is, by amazing grace, an essential element in God's redeeming purpose—so much so that without it the failure of its accomplishment may lie at our door."* ~ Andrew Murray

Prayers of Intercession

"Pray for each other so that you may be healed. The prayer of a righteous man is powerful and effective" (James 5:16 NIV).

The story is told of a young girl who said, "Lord, I am not going to pray for myself today; I am going to pray for others." But at the end of her prayer she added, "And please give my mother a handsome son-in-law!"

We just can't seem to end a prayer without asking something for ourselves. However, when we become disciplined enough to pray for others, we become partners with God in His work of salvation, healing, comfort, and justice. Of course, God can accomplish those things without us, but in His plan we are given the privilege of being involved with Him through prayer.

When we intercede for someone in trouble, facing surgery, who needs Christ, has lost a loved one, or a pastor who needs strength, we are asking God to provide for that person what we cannot give them ourselves. We are interceding for God to direct His power in a specific direction for a specific person for a specific reason/need.

Prayer is not a magic wand for satisfying our own desires and wishes, but it's a God-given opportunity to work with the

Lord in accomplishing His purposes. *"This is the confidence which we have before Him, that if we ask anything according to His will, He hears us"* (1 John 5:14 NIV).

You may not feel like praying for others because you are so in need of prayer yourself. However, there is a basic truth about God's kingdom, we find healing for ourselves by ministering on behalf of others. Many of us go to church looking for healing that will make us whole and make us more effective ministers for our Lord.

But Jesus wants us to get out there, with all of our own needs, and minister to others. When we do this, it's amazing how we will find the needed healing and strength which we're seeking! Fervent intercessory prayer for others that comes from a pure heart will result in God doing mighty things in the lives of both the intercessor and the one for whom he/she is interceding.

Dec 30

Chuckle: *What's the difference between a cat and a comma? A cat has its claws at the end of its paws; a comma is a pause at the end of a clause.*

Quote: *"If you are too busy to spend time alone with God, you are busier then God intends for you to be."* ~ Unknown Author

Believe and Receive

"When you ask, you must believe (have faith) and not doubt" (James 1:6 NIV). Jesus said, *". . . whatever you ask for in prayer, believe (have faith) that you have received it and it will be yours"* (Mark 11:24 NIV).

Think back with me to yesterday. From the time you awoke until you went to bed last night, how many times did you feel inadequate and lacking in wisdom to deal with a situation you were facing? If after careful reflection on this question, you answer "none," then you probably went through the day depending upon your own strength and wisdom to make decisions and deal with issues that arose. You see, even if we think we know the best answer to a problem, or the best way to handle a situation, we are settling for second best wisdom—ours.

In our first passage, James is referring to prayer for wisdom. However, when we ask God for wisdom, or anything, we must believe and not doubt. From our two passages, we see that believing (having faith) is essential for God to answer our prayers and grant our requests. Faith is believing God and acting on that faith. "If God says it, I believe it, and I will ask Him!" When you pray, do you do so with confidence that God will answer, or is prayer just one more possibility among other resources you depend upon to handle life situations? Maybe you pray something like this: "OK, Lord, I'm asking, but I don't really think you will answer my prayer." What kind of faith is that? A doubting Christian is one who says he trusts God, but really trusts himself or someone else more. He says he has faith, but he really doesn't.

A doubting mind is not completely convinced that God's way is best. Such a person makes God's Word just like human advice and retains the option to disregard or disobey it. This kind of person vacillates between allegiance to his subjective feelings, the world's ideas, and God's commands. He is divided inside. He is "double-minded." *"That person (without faith) should not think he will receive anything from the Lord; he is a double-minded person, unstable in all he does"* (James 1:7-8 NIV).

A double-minded Christian is one who knows Christ as Savior and is going to heaven, but on a daily basis does not have the faith to trust God in all situations and depend upon His divine wisdom to guide his life. We can pray all night to no avail unless we believe God and take Him at His word. *"Without faith, it is impossible to please God"* (Hebrews 11:6 NIV).

A pastor said this: *"True wisdom enables us to do the right thing in the face of moral dilemmas and to interpret life's experiences in light of eternal values."* Only God can grant this true wisdom for living.

If we pray with God's will uppermost in our minds, our prayers will be pleasing to Him and we can express our desires to Him with the expectation that He will answer.

Dec 31

Chuckle: *A woman went to a marriage counselor and complained of her husband's overwhelming self-interest. "It was evident from the minute we married," she said. "He even wanted to be in the wedding pictures."*

Quote: *"If you truly love Him, your service for Him in the new year will be of the quality that He desires."* ~ Henry Blackaby

A Wonderful Year

"Come to me, all you who are weary and burdened, and I will give you rest. Take my yoke upon you and learn from me, for I am gentle and humble in heart, and you will find rest for your souls. For my yoke is easy and my burden is light" (Matthew 11:28-30 NIV).

If you love the Christmas season as much as I do, you wish it would never end. But for Christians, the spirit of Christmas need never end. Our joy should continue all year long just from reflecting on the love of God that has given us eternal life through faith in the crucified and risen Babe of Bethlehem. With the passing of Christmas, our minds logically turn to the new year. Let's listen to God as we prepare our hearts for the coming year.

There's a story about a happy little boy with tremendous confidence.

"Cocking his bat, he tossed the ball into the air, saying, "I'm the greatest batter in the world!" Then he swung and missed. "Strike one," he said. He picked up the ball, examined it, and then threw it into the air again. As he swung, he repeated, "I'm the greatest batter in the world." Once again he missed. "Strike two," he said. This time, he stopped to examine his bat to make sure

there wasn't a hole in it. Then he picked up the ball, adjusted his cap, and tossed the ball into the air for the third time, and again said, "I'm the greatest batter in the world," and swung with all his might—and missed for the 3rd straight time. "Wow" he cried, "What a pitcher. I'm the greatest pitcher in the world!"

Are you a great batter or a great pitcher? One thing is for sure, at times we have all struck out. It's good to start over afresh with the new year. As you face a new year, you may be painfully remembering how you failed your Lord in the past year. Maybe you were not faithful to His calling on your life. Maybe you lived a life of disobedience. Like the little boy, may I suggest that your attitude will largely determine whether the new year is a year of victory or a year of defeat.

In our basic passage, God calls us to consciously decide to come to Him for comfort and rest, and to learn from him—learn to have His attitude about life, love, and service to others. Jesus said, *"I have come that they (you and I) may have life, and have it to the full"* (John 10:10 NIV). He's talking about life in the here and now as well as in eternity. We all enter the New Year asking, "What will it mean to me?" "What can I do with it?" These are natural new year thoughts. We don't know what the future holds but we know who holds the future and that the new year will be what we allow God to make of it.

Without a promise of tomorrow, we can plan, with God's help, to make the coming year the best year of our lives. *"If this is to be a Happy New Year, a year of usefulness, a year in which we shall live to make this earth better, it is because God will direct our pathway. How important then, to feel our dependence upon Him!"* ~ Matthew Simpson

About the Author:

Jerry Stratton grew up as the son of a Baptist minister in the beautiful mountains of Northwest Arkansas. He is a graduate of Ouachita Baptist University, Arkadelphia, Arkansas; and Baylor University, Waco, Texas. He served in the U.S. Army for a total of 30 years and retired in December, 1984.

Upon retirement from the army, Jerry sensed God's call to vocational ministry. In his 28 years of ministry, he has served as minister of education and administration, director of missions, pastor, and interim pastor. For the past eight years, he has published a daily devotional via e-mail and his personal blog. In addition to his internet devotional ministry, Jerry continues to minister through his local church and substitute preaching.

Jerry and his wife, Dotse, met at Ouachita Baptist University. The celebrated 61 years of marriage in August, 2015 and make their home in Copperas Cove, Texas. Their two wonderful children have blessed them with six fantastic grandchildren.